**Brooklyn**
# BrewShop's

# BEER MAKING BOOK

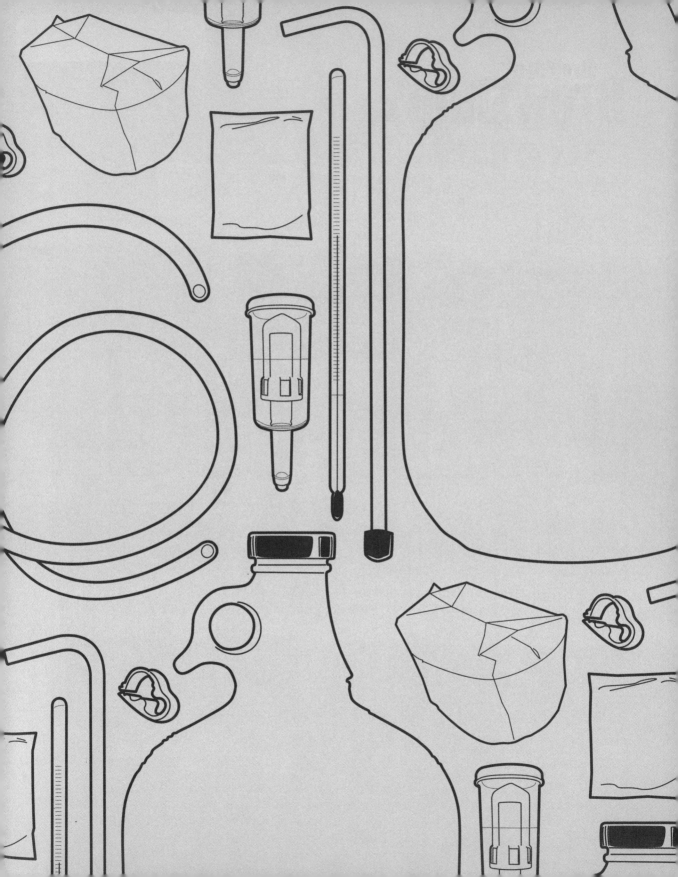

# Brooklyn BrewShop's

# BEER MAKING BOOK

**52 SEASONAL RECIPES FOR SMALL BATCHES**

**ERICA SHEA & STEPHEN VALAND** WITH JENNIFER FIEDLER

ILLUSTRATIONS BY DERYCK VONN LEE

**CLARKSON POTTER/PUBLISHERS**
**NEW YORK**

Copyright © 2011 BY ERICA SHEA and STEPHEN VALAND
Illustrations copyright © 2011 by Deryck Vonn Lee

All rights reserved.
Published in the United States by Clarkson Potter/Publishers,
an imprint of the Crown Publishing Group,
a division of Random House, Inc., New York.
www.crownpublishing.com
www.clarksonpotter.com

CLARKSON POTTER is a trademark and POTTER with
colophon is a registered trademark of Random House, Inc.

Library of Congress Cataloging-in-Publication Data
is available upon request.

ISBN 978-0-307-88920-1
eISBN 978-0-307-88921-8

Printed in the United States of America

BOOK DESIGN by Laura Palese
COVER DESIGN by Laura Palese
COVER ILLUSTRATION by Deryck Vonn Lee

10  9  8  7  6  5

First edition

# CONTENTS

**CONTENTS CONTINUE ➡**

# INTRO

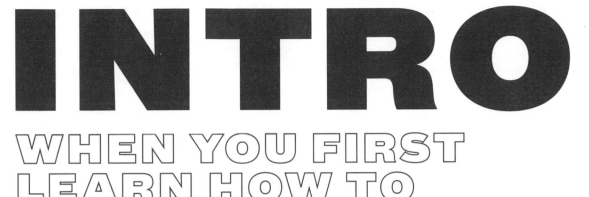

## WHEN YOU FIRST LEARN HOW TO COOK, YOU FOLLOW EVERY INSTRUCTION IN A RECIPE.

You buy full jars of spices, prep all the ingredients, preheat the oven, and then run back to the store to pick up that one item you forgot. And you worry, maybe, that you didn't add enough salt. What is a "pinch" anyway? But when you take the roasted pork chops out of the oven or taste your butternut squash soup and realize that you've made a meal that's not only edible but also delicious, it's magic.

- - - - - - - - - - - - - - - - - - - - - - - - - - - - - - - - - - - - - - - - - - - - -

So you do it again. You discover that oil works instead of butter. Or that toasting pine nuts really does make a difference in flavor and that you don't need to check the thermometer to know when to take a chicken out of the oven. You stop reading the recipes and, instead, make up your own.

That's what brewing beer is like, too. The first time, it's magic. It's alcohol. It's carbonated. And you made it in your kitchen. But after you have a few batches under your belt, you see how it all works and can start to play around.

## WE STARTED MAKING BEER

after Erica unearthed an old glass carboy from her father's basement, a relic from his brief foray into brewing some fifteen years earlier.

We loved to eat, and as recent college graduates, we didn't like the idea of being broke in New York City, so we cooked. We started making ice cream from scratch and then fresh pasta. We found that what we made was better than anything we could find on grocery store shelves. When we inherited the brewing equipment, beer seemed like a natural choice for our next project.

For a month, we read brewing books and websites, trying to understand the process, the vocabulary, and the science. It was intimidating. What was "acidulation"? What was "fluctuation"? But when we actually turned on the stove, we discovered a funny thing: Making beer was easy.

Beer is made from just four basic ingredients: grains, hops, yeast, and water. You steep the grains in hot water to extract their sugars, strain and discard the grains, and then boil the collected liquid with hops to get the right flavor. After that, the yeast does most of the work. It eats the sugar left over from the grain to produce alcohol and carbon dioxide.

Our beer was not just any beer—it was good beer. Some of the recipes in this book originated from these early trials. Our Grapefruit Honey Ale (page 68) was one of the first beers we created and is still one of our most popular and requested recipes.

So we kept at it. Making beer in our kitchen in small batches had advantages to buying beer on store shelves. We used the same process that breweries do, just scaled down, and we had access to the same high-quality grains, hops, and yeast. But since we were making beer for just the two of us, we could use ingredients that might be cost-prohibitive for a larger operation. For a brewery, honey and maple syrup are a lot more expensive than corn sugar, but we already had those in our cupboard. And we could use herbs from our kitchen garden or berries that we picked up at the greenmarket instead of lesser-quality syrups and extracts.

**TAKE A TRIP TO ANY OF THE REALLY BIG BREWERIES IN AMERICA** and you'll notice something strange: They look like a place that would more likely produce high-grade plastics than beer. Brewing wasn't always something done in industrial-size tanks with top-grade scientific equipment. It was a craft. Monks brewed beer. Women brewed beer. It was part of running a kitchen in the seventeenth and eighteenth centuries because drinking beer meant not dying from drinking contaminated water.

In northern Europe (where most styles of beer on shelves today originated) differing climates and local ingredients made for regional variations. In Belgium, brewing with wheat, sugars, and spices produced hazy witbiers, complex saisons, and high-alcohol tripels. In Germany, a grain shortage that threatened food stocks led to the passage of the Beer Purity Law of 1516 (Reinheitsgebot), stating that in most cases, beer could only be made from barley, hops, and water. Crisp lagers, malty amber bocks, and rich, dark dunkels were the result. Robust porters came from England, farmhouse ales from France, and red ales from Ireland.

European brewing styles came to America with the colonists. Pilgrims made beer out of pumpkins, spruce, and corn when stocks of traditional grains ran low. Even the founding fathers brewed beer; one of George Washington's recipes called for wheat bran and molasses. By the nineteenth century, there were more than 4,000 active small, local breweries—well over two times as many as there are today.

The swift one-two of Prohibition and the industrialization of all things edible, however, knee-capped independent brewers. Beer production became concentrated in a few hands, making bland, watered-down lagers the standard for what America had to offer.

In 1978, when he wasn't nailing solar panels to the White House roof, President Jimmy Carter signed the bill that lifted restrictions on home brewing, and things began to change as local independent breweries sprang up by the handful and people who loved craft beer started to brew their own at home.

A lot has happened in the beer world since the seventies. The big breweries have grown even bigger, but so too has the world of independent craft breweries. Beer has become big business. Some big beer factories don't even use real hops anymore; some craft breweries use more than ever.

But the most important thing has been the reemergence of beer as an artisanal craft. Today beer belongs on the dinner table, not just in front of the television or at tailgates. Craft beer is on the beverage list at Thomas Keller's French Laundry. Great beer can be purchased in supermarkets and corner stores and is available in refillable growlers. The number of small breweries in the United States has grown from 1,147 in 2000 to over 1,700 in 2011.

But for some, the idea of brewing beer at home still seems out of reach. We know this because of the questions we were asked when people first found out we brewed beer. "Do you make it in your bathtub?" was usually the first question, followed by either "Does it smell?" or "Do you have a huge apartment?" To which, the answers were no, no, and no.

- - - - - - - - - - - - - - - - - - - - - - - - - -

**AFTER TASTING OUR BEERS,** our friends wanted to know how to make their own. Some of them couldn't believe that we had made real beer, something they would pay money for in a bar (even eight dollars a pint in New York City). Looking around, we realized that the city that had a million of everything didn't have a single brewing supply store. In this food-obsessed metropolis, we figured there had to be people who wanted to brew but either didn't think they had the space or didn't want their kitchens looking or smelling like a brewery.

We brainstormed a way to brew on a smaller scale and to make it more like cooking. We fashioned a one-gallon kit out of sawed-down and hand-drilled parts from larger five-gallon kits. We worked out a recipe and gave it a shot.

It was perfect. We cut an hour off the process. Our one-gallon batches heated up and cooled down much faster than the five-gallon ones. There was less mess and Erica could actually lift everything. We had enough burners to make three one-gallon batches at a time. And the one-gallon batch made 10 bottles' worth, which lasted just long enough for us to think up our next beer.

We figured out a way to brew in a tiny kitchen, and we couldn't wait to show other people how to do this as well. On Fourth of July weekend in 2009, we started the Brooklyn Brew Shop at the Brooklyn Flea, a quirky market mixing vendors of artisanal pickles, locally designed jewelry, used records, vintage furniture, and whatever else you can think of. We offered three items: a one-gallon equipment kit that we designed especially for urban apartments, and two ingredient mixes, Grapefruit Honey Ale (page 68) and Chocolate Maple Porter (page 138). Five-gallon kits and mixes, for parties and larger kitchens, would be added in a few weeks. Our goal was to make brewing straightforward, fun, easy, and—most important—delicious.

The first few weekends at the Brooklyn Flea were marathon teaching sessions as we got so many questions—not to mention curious looks from people who didn't even know brewing at home was legal, never mind easy. Word of mouth turned into local press, which attracted national media, which meant shipping across the country. We moved our "office" from Stephen's apartment to a loft in downtown Brooklyn and then to a 6,000-square-foot warehouse, all in just 14 months.

We added new recipes as the seasons changed, taking cues from local greenmarkets for inspiration. Fall apples from upstate turned into an Apple Crisp Ale (page 102). Roasted pumpkin was added to a Belgian abbey-style dubbel (see page 124). For the holidays, when the smell of roasted nuts is inescapable on busy New York City streets, we made a Chestnut Brown Ale (page 140).

By now, we have made thousands of test batches. We've helped people buy kits as favors for bachelor parties, presents for Dad, housewarming gifts, and rainy-day projects. Culinarily inclined couples who want to try something new pick up multiple mixes at a time. Our customers have started to experiment with our recipes, too, and they often stop by the market to bring us bottles to try. Instead of grapefruit, they'll use ginger. Cherries for blackberries. Hazelnuts for chestnuts. They take our recipes and make them their own.

In that spirit, we wanted to create a book with our best recipes. We picked our best-selling but never-before-published recipes, plus our favorites that we made just for ourselves and our friends. We arranged the recipes as we make them: by season. As you work your way through this book, you should be able to not only brew our beers but also make up your own. We hope that you have as much fun as we have had. Now, make some beer.

HAPPY BREWING!
ERICA & STEPHEN

# EQUIPMENT

## WHEN PEOPLE ASK US WHAT THEY NEED TO START BREWING

besides what comes in our kit, we say that if you've ever made a pot of pasta, you're in pretty good shape. With a stockpot, strainer, and funnel, you're almost ready to brew. You'll just need a few more pieces. The standard size for making beer at home is five gallons. That makes 50 bottles at a time, which is great for a party, but for small kitchens and apartments, we recommend brewing one gallon at a time, which yields up to 10 bottles. This book focuses on one-gallon batches. If you want to start small and go big later on, it's easy. Just take a look at the list below to make sure you have everything you'll need to start making your first batch of beer.

- - - - - - - - - - - - - - - - - - - - - - - - - - - - - - - - - - - - - - - - - - - - - -

### IN OUR KIT
### (see Sources, page 172)

**AIRLOCK:** During fermentation, this plastic contraption lets carbon dioxide out of the fermenter while keeping beer-killing bacteria and contaminants from getting in. We like the basic three-piece chambered version (with base, interior cap, and lid).

**FERMENTER:** During fermentation, beer needs to rest in a nonreactive covered container while the yeast is working. We use glass because it's neutral and easy to clean, but you may also come across plastic or stainless-steel options. Plastic can harbor bacteria in the scuffed-up parts along its walls that can then impart off-flavors if the beer is left there too long. And since glass is clear, you'll be able to check on your beer's progress throughout fermentation. This will make you a better brewer in the long run as you learn what to look for. For one gallon, you'll be using a one-gallon glass jug. For bigger batches, a five-gallon glass carboy will do.

**RACKING CANE:** Similar to what you may find in any gas thief or aquarium enthusiast's tool chest, this rigid J-shaped tube will be part of your operation to siphon beer out of the fermenter and into bottles. A length of 16 inches will be long enough for a one-gallon-size fermenter; go up to 24 inches for five gallons. Alternatively, consider upgrading to an **auto-siphon,** which you can use instead of a racking cane. You'll then be able to start a siphon with a single pump instead of the balancing act involved in using a racking cane to make a gravity siphon (see page 31).

**SANITIZER:** We recommend a food-grade no-rinse sanitizer so it won't wreck your beer if some residue ends up in your bottles. Star San and One-Step are our favorites. C-Brite is a great rinse cleanser. Follow the manufacturer's instructions to make a cleaning solution. Keeping some on hand in a spray bottle can be quite handy when brewing.

**SOFT TUBING:** Three and a half to four feet of 5/16-inch-diameter clear plastic food-grade tubing will be perfect for brewing. For a five-gallon batch, you'll also need a three-foot length of one-inch-diameter vinyl food-grade tubing. When your beer is fermenting for the first few days, the yeast produces lots of carbon dioxide—sometimes enough to push the stopper off of your fermenter or clog your airlock. This tubing will help to channel the gas out quickly while keeping your operation bacteria-free.

**STOPPER:** This covers the mouth of the fermenter. When we first introduced our one-gallon kits we included a rubber stopper and hard plastic attachment that we originally had to saw by hand. It worked well but we got tired of sawing. Now we include a screw-cap stopper with a hole that fits both tubing (see opposite) and an airlock (see opposite). For five gallons, use a rubber stopper with a hole drilled through it or a molded plastic plug (carboy bung).

**THERMOMETER:** You'll need a thermometer that can register temperatures as low as 70°F and as high as 200°F. We use a laboratory thermometer that's 12 inches long, to keep our hands away from the heat.

**TUBING CLAMP:** This little clip slides onto the soft tubing and, when clenched, forms a seal to keep liquid from flowing out so you can fill one beer bottle at a time.

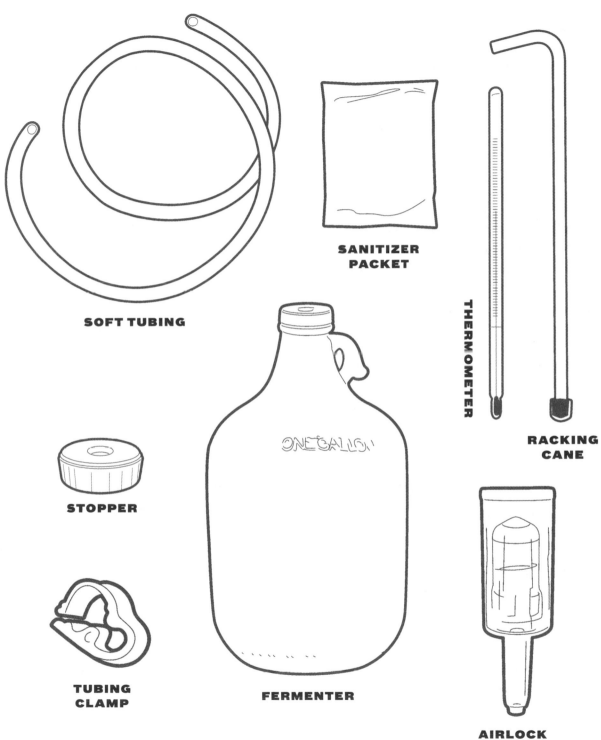

SOFT TUBING

SANITIZER PACKET

THERMOMETER

RACKING CANE

STOPPER

TUBING CLAMP

FERMENTER

AIRLOCK

# IN YOUR KITCHEN

**FINE-MESH STRAINER:** For a one-gallon batch, the ideal strainer is sturdy, stainless steel, and large enough (8 to 10 inches in diameter) to hold all the grain at once. You'll be pouring hot water through it, so having a resting ring that allows you to hook it onto the rim of your bowl or pot is a bonus.

A kitchen strainer works for smaller batches, but unless it can hold 12 pounds of wet grain at once (unlikely), for five gallons consider upgrading to a reusable nylon mesh sparging bag and a 6.5-gallon plastic bucket with a spigot that you can strain all your liquid into at once.

**FUNNEL:** This will make your life easier when it comes to pouring beer into the fermenter. Contact with the beer is quick and minimal, so plastic and metal are both fine. We use an eight-inch funnel. It's big and funny looking, but any size is better than no funnel at all, so whatever you have in your kitchen should work. Funnels with a strainer or screen attachment are a bonus.

**SCALE:** A lot of brewing supply stores sell ingredients only by the pound (grain) or ounce (hops). A scale is useful for measuring out smaller amounts.

**STOCKPOTS:** For one gallon of beer, a pot that holds six quarts will do. Twenty percent of the beer evaporates when boiling, so you need a pot that holds more than the one gallon you'll end up with. A second pot of a similar size is handy if you have it—otherwise you can get away with a quick rinse and a large mixing bowl for the sparge step (see page 26). For five gallons, use two large stockpots (or one giant one). You'll need to be able to boil 6.5 gallons at a time. We prefer to split a five-gallon batch over two pots because everything heats and cools faster and is easier to move. Unless you frequent chili cook-offs or host lobster boils regularly, it's also easier to justify having multiple smaller pots than one big cauldron.

**TIMER:** You'll need something to keep track of time. We use the timer on our cell phone.

# BOTTLING

**BOTTLE CAPPER:** A few models are available. There are automated ones like you'll find in a brewery, cappers you clamp to a table and operate with one hand so that you can presumably drink with the other, and stand-alone models that ram corks into your bottles in one quick drill-press motion. We've found that the basic two-handed double-lever versions work well. We still use the one recovered from Erica's basement, and the design hasn't changed in more than twenty years.

**BOTTLE CAPS:** Keep a couple bags of crown caps on hand. If kept dry, they don't go bad.

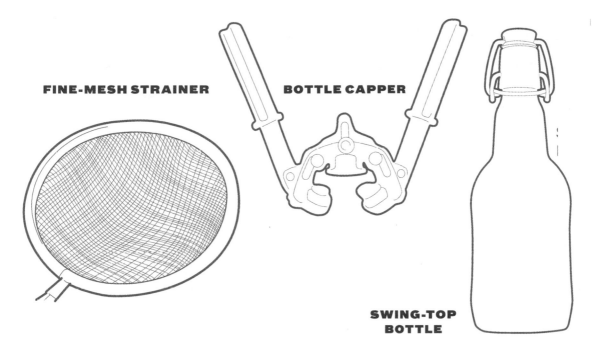

**FINE-MESH STRAINER**

**BOTTLE CAPPER**

**SWING-TOP BOTTLE**

**BOTTLES:** Reuse beer bottles with swing-top or non-twist-off closures. If you have swing-top bottles, such as the kind used by Grolsch, you won't need bottle caps or a capper. We recommend buying beers and drinking while brewing; it's the fun part of recycling.

# MEASURING ALCOHOL BY VOLUME

Every recipe is listed with the approximate Alcohol by Volume (ABV) based on the amount of fermentable sugars in the recipe. You can usually tell when your beer is finished fermenting by looking. If you've waited the allotted two weeks and the surface is free of bubbles, the beer's color has deepened, and the yeast has settled to the bottom of the fermenter—thereby clarifying your beer—it is most likely ready to be bottled. But if you want to know for sure that your beer is finished fermenting, you can buy a **hydrometer,** which measures the density of liquids.

A hydrometer will tell you if the yeast in the beer has finished converting the sugars from the grains to alcohol. It will come with instructions, but in general, you take one measurement before you add the yeast to tell you how much sugar is in the liquid (original gravity) and one measurement when you think fermentation is finished (final gravity). If the ABV is falling short of what is listed in the recipe, let the beer keep fermenting.

# INGREDIENTS

## BEER IS MADE FROM FOUR ESSENTIAL INGREDIENTS:

Grains, hops, yeast, and water. The following is a guide to these ingredients and how they work. At a good brewing supply store, you'll be able to grab almost everything you need in one swoop—either in person or online. Most of these ingredients won't go bad in transit, so you can have them shipped to you without a problem. If you're ordering liquid yeast, which is highly perishable, request an ice pack to keep it cool. For Sources, see page 172.

- - - - - - - - - - - - - - - - - - - - - - - - - - - - - - - - - - - - - - - - -

## GRAIN

It's an age-old story. Grain meets hot water. Grain loses its sugar to hot water. Brewers throw grain away and make beer out of the sugary hot liquid that's left.

A lot of grain goes into making beer. For every pint, you'll need around three-quarters of a pint glass worth of grain. But it's not really the grain that brewers want, it's the sugar inside. This sugar gets converted to alcohol by the yeast, so the more grain you use, the more alcohol your beer will have.

When we say "grain," we almost always mean barley. Of all the cereal grains, barley has the most maltose (the type of sugar that yeast likes to eat) and also a strong husk that makes a natural filter. Wheat and rye are also used, but less often and usually in addition to a barley base.

Barley destined for the brew pot is usually malted before it reaches a brewing supply store. Remember sprouting beans in paper towels in elementary-school science class? If, instead of watching the bean grow, you had put it in the oven once the roots started popping out, then you would have been malting. This heating process makes the maltose sugars inside the grain more accessible. The same sugar is what makes malted milk balls and malted milkshakes taste so good. It's also the reason the grains used in beer are referred to as "malts."

During the malting process, grains are heated to various degrees to bring out different flavors. The more the grains are roasted, the less sugar they have to convert to alcohol. Most beer recipes include a combination of grains: the lightest, least roasted grains (base malts) are used to add body and alcohol, while the more roasted grains (specialty malts) add flavor and color.

Kilned malts are the lightest of the specialties and provide notes of bread and nuts. Caramel malts add colors ranging from honey to mahogany and leave a residual toffee-like sweetness. Roasted malts give beer a chocolate or coffee flavor and a deep, dark hue.

**Note:** Before you begin brewing, you'll need to get your grains milled so that it's possible to extract the maltose trapped inside the tough husk. What you want is a cracked, coarse texture—too fine of a grind and you'll get malted barley flour. Brewing supply stores will do this for you.

## GLUTEN-FREE RECIPES

For the gluten-sensitive, there are ways to get around brewing with traditional grains. You'll find tips for working with alternate grains and starchy vegetables in our four gluten-free recipes.

- **G-F CARROT-PILS** (page 60)
- **G-F BEET-BUCKWHEAT ALE** (page 92)
- **G-F PUMPKIN DUBBEL** (page 127)
- **G-F GINGERBREAD ALE** (page 163)

**Note:** When brewing gluten-free beers, be sure to use dried yeast. The liquid yeasts are cultivated from beer and may include gluten.

# BASE MALTS

**AMERICAN 2-ROW:** These tiny pale malts pack a lot of sugar that is easily converted to alcohol. "Two-row" is a standard term that refers to a specific cultivar of barley that has two rows of seeds on the stem. It's considered better for most beer styles than "6-row" barley, which has more protein.

**ENGLISH PALE:** This is the English version of basic "two-row" malt, which is just a bit more sweet and malty than the American style because it's usually kilned at a higher temperature. It provides a light amber color and a slightly nutty flavor.

**MARIS OTTER:** Kilned just a touch longer than most base malts, this barley cultivar, which was developed at Cambridge, England, in the 1960s, forms the familiar malty, nutty backbone to many British pale ales and mild ales. **Golden Promise** is a Scottish malt that is similar, with a slightly sweeter flavor.

**MUNICH:** In small amounts, this German-style malt adds a golden amber color and a slight malty flavor. When used as the majority of the grain, it produces a darker color and more pronounced maltiness found in German-style bocks or Oktoberfests. **Dark Munich,** or "Munich II," has been kilned longer and is better for darker beers.

**PILSNER:** This efficient malt is one of the lightest and most commonly used for pale German, Belgian, and Eastern European lagers and ales.

# SPECIALTY MALTS

**AROMATIC:** In small amounts, this adds outsized doses of malty flavor and aroma, as well as an orange to copper color.

**BISCUIT:** There is a moment when you're baking bread or pastries in the oven just before they are done when that toasted aroma fills the room. This lightly roasted malt re-creates those notes in beer, but it needs a solid base malt to work with; it's not terribly efficient on its own.

**BLACK PATENT:** Just a tiny amount of these dark malts—the darkest of all the malts—will add coffee-like, roasted notes to porters and stouts.

**CARA-PILS:** This is malt that's been kilned in a special way so that it adds a nice fluffy head on the finished beer and adds body without affecting flavor or aroma.

**CHOCOLATE:** These malts get their name from their dark brown color, but the flavor isn't that far off from chocolate. Think more raw cocoa than candy bars, though—roasted, earthy notes with just a touch of bitterness.

**CRYSTAL OR CARAMEL:** These add sweet notes of honey and caramel as well as color ranging from golden to dark brown. They are available on a sliding scale of roastiness from light (10) to dark (120).

**PALE WHEAT:** A handful of these malted grains will help with obtaining a fluffy white head without changing the flavor or aroma of the beer, but when used as a larger percentage of the recipe, these form the hazy, bready core of wheat beers. **Torrified wheat** (wheat grains that have been heated quickly to puff them up) is used in small doses to help with head retention as well.

**ROASTED BARLEY:** Because these super-dark grains are not malted, they don't add a lot of fermentable sugar but do leave a deep color and almost a burnt-toast flavor that can be terrific in porters and stouts.

**SMOKED:** Instead of being cooked in an oven, smoked malts are dried over burning wood, creating a smokiness not unlike the one that clings to your clothes after sitting by a campfire. The smoked grains capture the character of the wood: **Peat** gives the earthy and diesel notes in scotch; **beechwood** lends a more intense, drier smoke aroma; and **cherrywood** gives a smooth and sweet character.

**SPECIAL B:** The key ingredient to many a Belgian dubbel, this dark caramel-type malt leaves a deep color, a baked-toffee aroma, and some raisiny sweetness.

**VICTORY®:** American maltster Briess makes this grain that adds warming nutty and biscuit aromas and full-bodied flavor without much sweetness.

**VIENNA:** Typical to German-style lagers, this malt adds a golden color and rich, malty flavor.

# HOPS

Hops are dried flower clusters that add bitterness and flavor to beer, and while they are now considered essential, it wasn't always the case. Medieval brewers included roots and herb blends, until they noticed that beers made with hops lasted longer. Turns out hops are a natural preservative.

The oils and resins in the dried hop flowers add bitterness, flavor, and aroma to beer depending on when they are added in the brewing process. Think of adding hops as something like adding herbs to a stew. If you add dried herbs in the beginning, their flavor will season and blend into the broth. If you add chopped herbs in the final minutes of preparation, they serve more as an aromatic accent.

**DRIED HOPS CAN GO STALE** if exposed to extreme temperatures or ultraviolet light. Make sure you buy hops that have been vacuum-sealed. To extend their freshness, store them in the fridge. Once opened, use within three months.

Although there are no absolute rules when it comes to choosing which hops to add to beer, some varieties (Columbus, Northern Brewer) work better as bittering agents. Those get added to boiling beer earlier to extract the maximum amount of bitterness. Other hops (Cascade, Hallertau, Saaz) are used for their flavor and aroma. Think citrusy, grassy, or floral notes. They often get added closer to the end of the boiling process to preserve their character. When you look at a recipe, you'll be able to tell which hop is doing what to your beer based on when it is added.

Varieties of hops can vary in bitterness from year to year and even from farm to farm. You'll be able to tell how bitter hops are when you purchase them by the alpha acid percentage (alpha acids are what make hops bitter). The higher the percentage, the more bitter the hop. Each style of hop has a typical alpha acid range and we've designed the recipes in this book with that in mind.

| HOPS | BITTERNESS* | DESCRIPTION |
| --- | --- | --- |
| **AMARILLO** (U.S.) | Medium to High | Grapefruit/Tart/Lively |
| **BRAMBLING CROSS** (U.K.) | Low | Black Currant/Lemon/Hay |
| **CASCADE** (U.S.) | Medium | Floral/Citrus/Pine |
| **CENTENNIAL** (U.S.) | High | Rounded/Pine/Tangerine |
| **CHALLENGER** (U.K.) | Medium | Spicy/Moss/Red Apple |
| **CHINOOK** (U.S.) | High | Pine/Black Pepper/Grapefruit |
| **CITRA** (U.S.) | High | Passion Fruit/Lime/Mango |
| **COLUMBUS** (U.S.) | High | Orange/Pine/White Flowers |
| **EAST KENT GOLDING** (U.K.) | Low to Medium | Dried Flowers/Moss/Plum |
| **FUGGLE** (U.K.) | Low | Dried Maple Wood/Wet Dirt/Old Man |
| **GLACIER** (U.S.) | Medium | Lemon Iced Tea/Licorice/Apricot |
| **HALLERTAU** (Germany) | Low | New Leaves/Crisp/Grassy |
| **NORTHERN BREWER** (U.S./Germany/U.K.) | Medium | Damp Forest/Mint/Pear |
| **PACIFIC JADE** (New Zealand) | High | Herbal/Fresh Citrus/Black Pepper |
| **PERLE** (Germany) | Medium | Pear/Mint/White Flowers |
| **SAAZ** (Czech) | Low | Dried Herbs/White Pepper/Apples |
| **SIMCOE** (U.S.) | High | Pine/Passion Fruit/Black Pepper |
| **SORACHI** (Japan) | High | Lemon Herbal Tea/White Flowers/Dust |
| **SPALTZ** (Germany) | Low | Crisp/Fresh/Ferns |
| **STYRIAN GOLDING** (Slovenia) | Low to Medium | White Pepper/Moss/Undergrowth |
| **TETTNANGER** (Germany) | Low | White Flowers/Straw/Peach |
| **WHITBREAD GOLDING** (U.K.) | Low | Red Apple/Wet Leaves/Fruitcake |
| **WILLAMETTE** (U.S.) | Low | Pear/Eucalyptus/Earth |

*In this chart, an average alpha acid between 0 and 6 percent constitutes "low," 6 to 9 percent is "medium," and above 9 is "high."

INTRO 21

Hops are sold in pellets, plugs, and whole-leaf form. All the recipes in this book call for pellets, which are dried hops that have been crushed and then re-formed into what looks like rabbit food. At that standard small size, you can better predict their effect on the beer, which is important when you're only making one gallon at a time. When substituting whole hops for hop pellets in this book, use 25 percent more.

**Note:** Hops are really cool plants to grow. To learn how, see page 34.

# YEAST

Yeasts are creepy and cool. They can lie dormant for months and then when introduced to some sweet unfermented beer they wake up, reproduce like mad, convert the sugars to alcohol, and then go dormant again. We like to say that yeasts do the hard work of making beer because they actually turn the beer into beer.

Before Louis Pasteur made the connection between yeast and fermentation in the nineteenth century, brewers didn't add yeast—they didn't know that yeast existed—but yeast was certainly in their beers. Wild yeast strains float like pollen in the air. If brewers left a tank of unfermented beer open, wild yeast would get in and get to work.

Gradually, brewers learned to control the addition of yeast. They reserved some of the sediment from the last batch of beer and threw it in the next batch, ensuring that the yeast would ferment the beer. They didn't know how it worked—they just knew it did—and like a sourdough starter, individual yeast strains were cultivated by breweries over hundreds of years.

Two main styles of yeast emerged and determined the differences between ales and lagers. Ale yeast, which works well at warmer temperatures (65°F to 75°F), ferments quickly and leaves a fruity taste. It hovers at the top of fermenting beer, creating a layer of foam. Lager yeast needs cool temperatures (46°F to 54°F), takes months to finish converting sugars, and works while sitting at the bottom, creating crisp, dry beers.

Yeast companies have identified many of the proprietary strains of popular styles of beer and produce generic versions. Each strain imparts its own particular characteristics, including flavor and aroma. Wheat beers get distinct banana and clove aromas from yeast. Belgian ale yeasts work at higher alcohol levels and can leave spicy notes, while American ale yeasts produce fruity flavors. German ale yeasts ferment dry and crisp. English ale yeasts allow the malty flavors from the grain to shine.

You can buy yeast in dried or liquid form. While all yeast should be stored in the fridge, dried yeast can survive on store shelves at moderate temperatures for months. Liquid yeast can last for six months in a refrigerator. Occasionally you can buy yeast straight from a brewery, too.

Yeast strains for home use are usually sold in packets designed for five-gallon batches. To scale down for a one-gallon batch, use half the packet. The yeast will multiply and then go to sleep and drop out as sediment once they've finished eating all the sugar.

**Note:** For each recipe in this book, we recommend both a general style of yeast and also a specific strain that we like for the particular recipe. If your brew shop is out of a certain strain, you can use a yeast within the general style.

## WATER

Beer will taste like the water that it's brewed with, so use water that you like to drink. We have great water in Brooklyn, so we use it straight from the tap. If you normally filter your drinking water then it's a good idea to do that for your brewing water as well. You don't want to use distilled water because its oxygen has been stripped out, leaving less fuel for the yeast.

## BELGIAN CANDI SUGAR

A type of rock candy that's derived from beets, Belgian Candi Sugar is the perfect meal for hungry yeast. Add some to your beer for a boost in alcohol without adding extra body. And contrary to what you might expect given the name, it will actually leave your beer tasting drier rather than sweeter.

**Note:** All instances of Belgian Candi Sugar in this book are for the clear variety. You might find dark or amber in your local brewing supply store. They will simply add a more toffee-like residual sweetness to your finished beer while increasing the alcohol.

# BEER STYLES

**WHEN WE COME UP WITH OUR BEERS,** our goal is to create something that will taste good and work well on the dinner table with food. Sometimes we start with a classic beer style in mind and riff on ingredients that would work well with that style (see Eggnog Milk Stout, page 160). Sometimes we find an ingredient that we really want to use, and search for a style that could showcase it (see Apple Crisp Ale, page 102). And sometimes we start from scratch to get something entirely new (see S'more Beer, page 82).

- - - - - - - - - - - - - - - - - - - - - - - - - - - - - - - - - - - - - - - - -

**PALE ALES AND AMBER ALES:** Born from the English brewing tradition, these ales range in color from pale straw to deep red and usually have a moderate amount of hop flavor and aroma. Amber ales are slightly maltier. See Tan (page 40), Tea & Toast (page 54), World's Greatest Dad Light (page 46), Grapefruit Honey Ale (page 68), and Gingerbread Ale (page 142).

**INDIA PALE ALES:** This heavily hopped English style developed in the eighteenth century and was brewed for long voyages to India and other colonies. It has become super-popular in America, where the bitterness quotient has been pushed higher and higher by intrepid craft breweries. See Everyday I.P.A. (page 36), Simcoe I.P.A. (page 74), and Rye P.A. (page 104).

**BROWN ALES:** These nutty, malty ales are a super-traditional English style that is usually light to dark brown in color with a sweet, roasted character. The classic versions are lightly hopped and moderate in alcohol. See World's Greatest Dad Brown (page 48), Mustard Brown Ale (page 122), and Chestnut Brown Ale (page 140).

**PORTERS AND STOUTS:** These dark English beers can come in a range of styles from sweet to bone-dry, chocolaty and mild to bitter and roasted. They're generally dark brown to black in color and are full-bodied, though not necessarily high in alcohol. See Black (page 38), World's Greatest Dad Dark (page 49), Peanut Butter Porter (page 110), Imperial Pepper Stout (page 108), Chocolate Maple Porter (page 138), Eggnog Milk Stout (page 160), and Coffee & Donut Stout (page 154).

**BELGIAN ALES:** Unfettered by brewing laws such as Germany's Reinheitsgebot (see page 8), Belgian brewers developed a tradition of incorporating spices, sugars, and fruits into their beers. The category covers a wide range of styles from the light, spicy saisons to the powerful abbey-style ales. See Rose-Cheeked & Blonde (page 42), Lady Lavender (page 44), Jalapeño Saison Mild (page 76), Jalapeño Saison Spicy (page 78), Lobster Saison (page 84), Bel-Gin Strong (page 88), Pumpkin Dubbel (page 124), Bourbon Dubbel (page 150), Honey Sage Seasonal (page 144), and New Year Beer (page 158).

**WHEAT BEERS:** Wheat grain makes up more than half the mix in a true wheat beer. Adding a handful of wheat to the grain mix brings a touch of haze and a bready aroma. The styles range from the light, fruity weisse beers and hefeweizens to the darker, maltier dunkelweizens. Common yeasts for wheat beers leave signature notes of cloves and bananas. See Edelweiss (page 58) and Cranberry Wheat (page 112).

**LAGER:** Cold-fermenting lager yeasts take longer to work and require cool storage, so we usually make ales instead. If you have a spare mini-fridge or a cool basement, however, the clean, crisp taste of a well-made lager is well worth the effort. See Spring Lager (page 56) and Oktoberfest (page 116).

**SPECIALTY:** Many beers defy easy categorization. From obscure regional styles to twists on traditional styles, the rest of the beers in our book stand on their own.

**A GREAT REFERENCE FOR MORE INFO ON BEER STYLES** is the Beer Judge Certification Program (www.BJCP.org). Even if you're not interested in becoming a professional beer judge, it publishes a thorough list of guidelines for some of your favorite styles, including some you've probably never heard of.

# SIX STEPS TO MAKING BEER

**THERE ARE SIX MAIN STEPS TO MAKING BEER.** First, steep the grains in hot water (**mash**), strain and discard the grains (**sparge**), boil the strained liquid with hops and spices (**boil**), then cool the liquid and add the yeast. Wait a few weeks as the yeast makes your beer for you (**fermentation**) and then bottle it with a little sugar for carbonation (**bottling**). The final step? Open a bottle and enjoy (**drinking**).

While it's better if you brew at the recommended temperatures and add all the ingredients at the exact time noted in the recipe, if you're off by a couple of degrees or behind by a few minutes, chances are your beer will come out just fine.

- - - - - - - - - - - - - - - - - - - - - - - - - - - - - - - - - - - - - - - - - - - - -

Brewing, like all avocations and hobbies, has developed its own jargon. We've kept it to a minimum in these instructions, and what we have included will help you talk shop with other brewers. So not only will you be ordering the best beers on tap, you'll also know exactly why they're so tasty.

Keeping your equipment sterile during brewing might be the most important thing you do. If your funnels, strainers, fermenter, tubes, and airlocks are not completely clean, your yeast can die or be overtaken by bacteria and wild yeast. Make a sanitizing solution (see page 12) and soak everything you're going to use according to the instructions for the sanitizer you're using.

# TO MAKE A ONE-GALLON BATCH

## STEP 1: THE MASH

Calculate how much water you'll need: one quart for every pound of grain in the recipe. In a medium stockpot, heat the water on the stove on high. When the temperature reaches 160°F, add all the grains (this is called "mashing in"). Stir gently with a spoon until "the mash" (the grains and the hot liquid) has the consistency of oatmeal. The temperature of the mash should reduce to 150°F within about a minute. Add tap water ¼ cup at a time if the mash looks too dry or the temperature is too high.

Turn off the heat, and let the grains steep uncovered for 60 minutes at a temperature of 144°F to 152°F. Any hotter and the grains will release unfermentable sugars, which will lead to a sweet nonalcoholic beer. Any cooler, and the grains won't release any sugars, which will give you barley-flavored water.

Stir every 10 minutes and use the thermometer to take the temperature of the mash from multiple locations. Turn on the heat if the temperature falls below the desired range. After 60 minutes, raise the heat to 170°F while stirring constantly (this is called "mashing out").

**Variation for five gallons:** Use a large stockpot that can hold up to 6.5 gallons of water.

## STEP 2: THE SPARGE

Place a fine-mesh strainer over a 6-quart pot (or large mixing bowl). Pour the mash into the strainer, reserving the collected liquid in the pot.

Heat additional water to 170°F. (If you have two stockpots, you can get this going while the mash is steeping.) Gently and evenly pour the sparging water over the grains (still resting over a pot or bowl). The liquid you've collected is called "wort." Recirculate the wort through the grains once. You're trying to extract as much flavor and sugars from the grains as possible.

**Variation for five gallons:** Line a 6.5-gallon plastic bucket with a sparging bag. Pour the mash into the bag, straining the liquid into the bucket. Heat additional water to 170°F. (If you have two large stockpots, you can get this going while the mash is steeping.) Pour the sparging water over the grains gently and evenly. Recirculate the wort through the grains once.

## STEP 3: THE BOIL

Return the pot with the wort to the stove on high heat. The beer will start to foam before reaching a boil (the "hot break"). Reduce the heat to a rolling boil and start a timer for 60 minutes. Add flavoring elements (hops, fruits, spices) at the times listed in the specific recipe. You will add some hops in the beginning of the boil for bitterness and some hops toward the middle and end for flavor and aroma.

## STEP 1: **THE MASH**

## STEP 2: **THE SPARGE**  ## STEP 3: **THE BOIL**

## STEP 4: FERMENTATION

Prepare an ice bath in your sink by plugging the drain and filling it with five inches of tap water and ice. After the boil is complete, cool the wort to 70°F, which will take around 30 minutes. Drain the water and refresh with new cold water and ice to make the process go faster. Using a sterilized funnel and a strainer, pour the cooled wort into a sanitized fermenter. Add any water needed to fill the fermenter to the one-gallon mark.

Add yeast to the wort according to the recipe's directions. Sanitize your hands. Shake the fermenter for at least two minutes, covering the open mouth with one clean hand. This will distribute the yeast evenly as well as aerate your wort. Oxygen will help fuel the yeast.

Plug the fermenter with the sanitized stopper. Make a "blow-off" tube by sticking the tubing into the hole in the stopper. Put the other end of the tube in a small bowl filled with sanitizing solution. This tube allows gas produced by the yeast converting the sugar to alcohol to get out, but allows nothing else in.

Store the fermenter somewhere dark and cool, like a closet. The bowl of sanitizer will begin to bubble as yeast consumes the sugars. Around two to three days later, the bubbling should slow from a fast and steady pace to an occasional blip. Replace the blow-off tube with an airlock.

**Variation for five gallons:** Since the five-gallon fermenter may be too heavy to shake, tilt it onto an edge and roll back and forth along the edge for two minutes.

# ASSEMBLING THE AIRLOCK

**A. ADD SANITIZER TO FILL LINE**

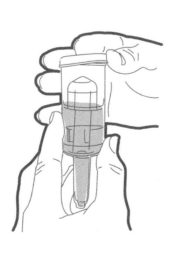

**B. CAP AIRLOCK**

**C. INSERT INTO STOPPER**

# STEP 4: FERMENTATION

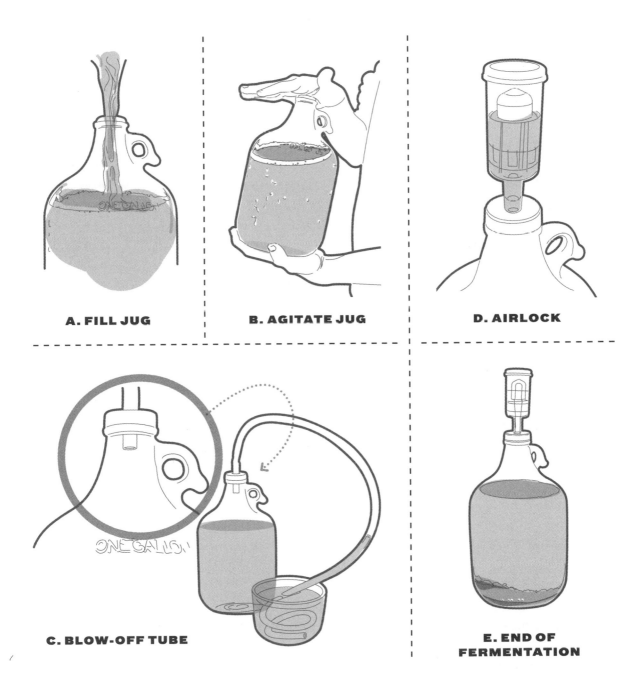

**A. FILL JUG**

**B. AGITATE JUG**

**D. AIRLOCK**

**C. BLOW-OFF TUBE**

**E. END OF FERMENTATION**

## STEP 5: BOTTLING

If you see bubbles on the surface of the beer two weeks from when you brewed, wait one more day and check again. When the surface looks clear, you're ready to bottle.

Prepare a sanitizing solution (see page 12). Thoroughly rinse 10 beer bottles, removing any sediment. Fill each bottle with enough sanitizing solution to swish around, then pour out the solution, letting the bottles dry upside down. If you're using no-rinse sanitizer, it's fine if there are a few bubbles from the solution left in the bottles when you fill them with beer. If you are using sanitizer that requires rinsing, though, make sure you wash it off completely.

Sanitize a medium stockpot and add the bottling sugar (usually honey or maple syrup) called for in the recipe. You want the sugar to be thin enough so that it will blend easily with the beer. If it's too sticky, add ½ cup water and heat on the stove on low heat, stirring until the honey or syrup has dissolved.

Put the full fermenter on a counter or table, being careful not to disturb the yeast sediment (called "trub") that has collected at the bottom. To get the beer out of the fermenter without disturbing the trub, you need to make a gravity siphon (practice using water if you've never done it before). You'll need a racking cane, 5/16-inch-diameter tubing, and a tube clamp. Attach the tubing clamp to one end of the tubing. Fill the tubing with sanitizing solution and clamp the tube shut. Attach the other end of the tubing to the short end of the sanitized racking cane. It should be a snug fit. Holding the tubing below the racking cane so it doesn't fill with sanitizing solution, remove the stopper on the jug and lower the racking cane into the beer, stopping just above the yeast sediment at the bottom.

With the free end of the tube over the sink or a small bowl, and with the end of the tube lower than the bottom of the racking cane, open the tubing clamp. Like magic, suction will force beer up through the racking cane and out of the tubing. Let the sanitizer flow into the sink or bowl until the beer begins to come out, then close the tubing clamp. Over the pot with the bottling sugar, release the clamp and let the beer flow, mixing with the sugar. Tilt the jug when the beer level gets low, but be careful not to suck up any of the yeast sediment in the process. Congratulations! You've mastered siphoning, an important aspect of simple mechanics.

Siphon the beer from the pot into the bottles with another gravity siphon, leaving one inch of headspace at the top of each bottle.

Using a bottle capper, seal your bottles with sanitized caps (if you're using swing-top bottles, close them). Let the beer sit in a cool dark place. The bottling sugar provides fuel to wake the yeast and carbonate your beer.

**Variation for five gallons:** Prepare 50 bottles instead of 10.

## STEP SIX: DRINKING

Two weeks after bottling, your beer will be ready to open. Chill and share with friends, if you're the sharing type.

# STEP 5: BOTTLING

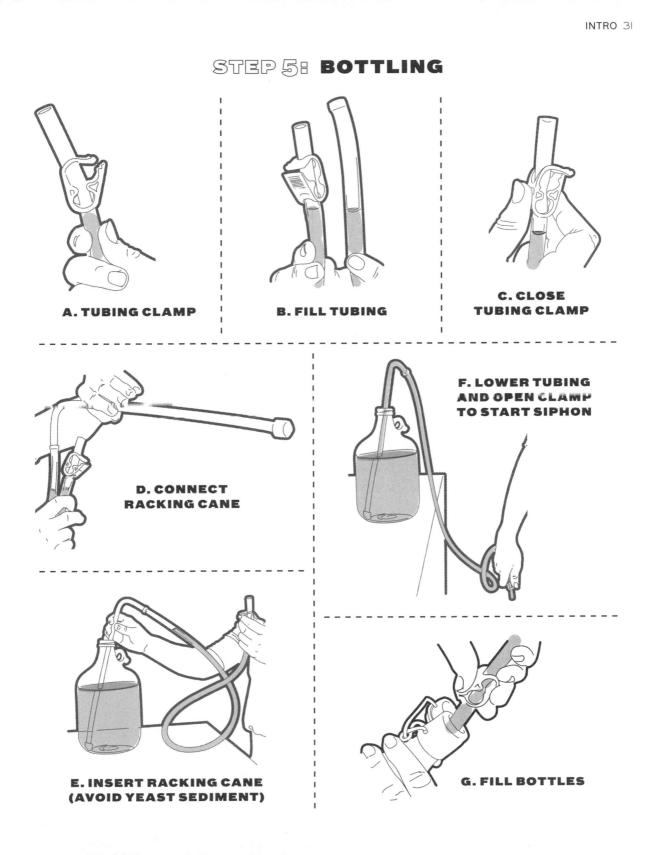

**A. TUBING CLAMP**

**B. FILL TUBING**

**C. CLOSE TUBING CLAMP**

**D. CONNECT RACKING CANE**

**F. LOWER TUBING AND OPEN CLAMP TO START SIPHON**

**E. INSERT RACKING CANE (AVOID YEAST SEDIMENT)**

**G. FILL BOTTLES**

# SPRING

## SPRING IS EAGERLY AWAITED AFTER A WINTER OF SLOSHING THROUGH COLD CITY STREETS.

It's the first time since fall when you can really enjoy being outside, and the greenmarkets start kicking again with potted herbs and pepper plants alongside the first peas and beans.

Springtime brewing is all about aromatics. From the first green shoots poking through the snow to lilacs and then roses, it's a cascading tumble of beautiful blooming things outside, and you want to capture that in your glass. Lighter beers start to emerge. Belgian blondes make great base beers for subtle floral elements or delicate herbs. We like to make fresh—and refreshing—beers to drink in the garden and to pair with the green vegetal produce from the farmer's markets. Late spring marks a parade of celebrations that call for large batches of beer, too—Mother's Day and Father's Day, graduations, weddings, and everything in between.

EVERYDAY I.P.A.
- - - - - - - - - - - - - - - - - - - - - - - - - - - - - - - - - - - - - - - - - - - - - -
BLACK & TAN
- - - - - - - - - - - - - - - - - - - - - - - - - - - - - - - - - - - - - - - - - - - - - -
ROSE-CHEEKED & BLONDE
- - - - - - - - - - - - - - - - - - - - - - - - - - - - - - - - - - - - - - - - - - - - - -
LADY LAVENDER
- - - - - - - - - - - - - - - - - - - - - - - - - - - - - - - - - - - - - - - - - - - - - -
WORLD'S GREATEST DAD LIGHT
- - - - - - - - - - - - - - - - - - - - - - - - - - - - - - - - - - - - - - - - - - - - - -
WORLD'S GREATEST DAD BROWN
- - - - - - - - - - - - - - - - - - - - - - - - - - - - - - - - - - - - - - - - - - - - - -
WORLD'S GREATEST DAD DARK
- - - - - - - - - - - - - - - - - - - - - - - - - - - - - - - - - - - - - - - - - - - - - -
CITRUS GOSE
- - - - - - - - - - - - - - - - - - - - - - - - - - - - - - - - - - - - - - - - - - - - - -
TEA & TOAST
- - - - - - - - - - - - - - - - - - - - - - - - - - - - - - - - - - - - - - - - - - - - - -
SPRING LAGER
- - - - - - - - - - - - - - - - - - - - - - - - - - - - - - - - - - - - - - - - - - - - - -
EDELWEISS
- - - - - - - - - - - - - - - - - - - - - - - - - - - - - - - - - - - - - - - - - - - - - -
GLUTEN-FREE CARROT-PILS
- - - - - - - - - - - - - - - - - - - - - - - - - - - - - - - - - - - - - - - - - - - - - -

BEER-BATTERED FRIED VEGETABLES
- - - - - - - - - - - - - - - - - - - - - - - - - - - - - - - - - - - - - - - - - - - - - -
LAVENDER SHORTBREAD WITH HONEY-BEER GLAZE

# SPRING FEATURE
# HOW TO GROW HOPS

Hops are flowers that grow on vines. At a hop farm, you'll see rows of leaning poles with dangling ropes where hop vines climb practically in front of your eyes (centimeters per day). They're one of the coolest plants for kids (or adults with short attention spans) to grow in a backyard because they grow so fast. If you're planting hops outdoors, late April is a good time. You want to wait until after the last frost, but still get them in the ground so they have lots of time to mature over the summer. In the spring, many brewing supply stores sell cuttings from hop plants, called rhizomes. You can check your local nursery or search online, too (see Sources, page 172). We've had success growing Chinook and Cascade hops in our loft. Here are some tips:

1 You'll need a growing space that gets lots of sun and has ample room for vertical growth since the plants can grow higher than 15 feet. They also develop pretty impressive root structures, so a backyard is ideal, but if you're in an apartment, it will work if you have super-high ceilings. Just use a really large planter. A five-gallon bucket with holes drilled in the bottom can work in a pinch.

2 Drainage is important. A mix of regular potting soil and nitrogen-rich compost (one with animal manure) will work best.

3 Dig a hole 4 inches deep and plant the rhizome horizontally.

4 Making a trellis can be as simple as hanging a rope from the ceiling to the plant. If you're growing outdoors, the hops should be against a wall where you can tie the string, or plant a sturdy pole. Bamboo works great. Tie the shoots to the string or pole until the vine begins to climb on its own.

5 Water when the dirt two inches below the surface feels dry. Be careful not to overwater because hops can be prone

to mold or insects, but if your hops begin to wilt, douse them with enough water to get down to the roots.

# HARVESTING HOPS

In autumn, the hop flowers will be fully developed. You'll be able to smell them. When they start to get papery around the edges, pick the entire cone. One fully mature hop plant should yield around a pound of flowers. Place the whole flowers on a tray in a single layer to dry out for a day or two out of direct sunlight. If you leave them in a jumble, they might develop mold. After the flowers are dried, put them in the freezer in a sealed plastic bag or plastic container until you are going to use them, and keep them away from light.

## PREPARING YOUR PLANT FOR WINTER

Hop vines are perennial, meaning they'll grow back every year if you treat them right. To winter them, cut them back to about three inches after the first frost and cover the stumps with dirt or compost. Come spring, the vines should pop out and be ready to go again. The plant will be almost twice as productive the second year, so if you have the space, it's a great investment.

# SINCE THE DAY WE OPENED FOR BUSINESS, our customers have asked for an India Pale Ale (I.P.A.)

recipe. It's not surprising: The extra-bitter, intensely hoppy beer has become one of the standards of the American craft brewing scene. Developed centuries ago in England and brewed for long overseas trips to colonies in India, this style of beer has extra hops that work as preservatives to help protect the beer from going bad.

Stephen came up with this I.P.A. for Brooklyn Brew Shop's first holiday season. It uses a combination of two hops: Columbus for the bitter base, then Cascade, the classic citrusy I.P.A. hop, added throughout the boil to preserve its flavor and aroma. We intended for the mix to be a special edition and even named it "Holiday I.P.A.," but come February, when we tried to replace it, people protested. Once we reached Valentine's Day and then Presidents' Day, it became clear we had to change the name. Luckily, this I.P.A. does work as an everyday beer: It's bitter but balanced, with a classic, bright and citrusy aroma and a strong malt backbone.

# EVERYDAY
# I.P.A. 6.8% ABV

## 60-MINUTE MASH AT 152°F

- 2½ quarts water, plus 1 gallon for sparging
- 1.8 pounds American 2-row malt
- 0.4 pound Caramel 20 malt
- 0.2 pound Victory malt
- 0.1 pound Munich malt
- *all grains should be milled (see note, page 17)

## 60-MINUTE BOIL

- 0.1 ounce Columbus hops
- 0.5 ounce Cascade hops, divided into fifths

## FERMENT

- ½ packet American ale yeast, such as Safale S-05 or Wyeast American Ale II (see note, page 22)
- 3 tablespoons honey, for bottling

**MASH:** In a medium stockpot, heat the 2½ quarts water over high heat to 160°F. Add all the malts and stir gently. The temperature should reduce to 150°F within 1 minute. Turn off the heat. Steep the grains for 60 minutes between 144°F and 152°F. Every 10 minutes, stir and take the temperature. If the grains get too cold, turn on the heat to high while stirring until the temperature rises to that range, then turn off the heat. With 10 minutes left, in a second medium stockpot heat the 1 gallon water to 170°F. After the grains have steeped for 60 minutes, raise the heat of the grains-and-water mixture to high and stir until the temperature reaches 170°F. Turn off the heat.

**SPARGE:** Place a fine-mesh strainer over a pot, and pour the grains into the strainer, reserving the liquid. Pour the 1 gallon of 170°F water over the grains. Recirculate the collected liquid through the grains once.

**BOIL:** Return the pot with the liquid to the stove on high heat and bring to a boil. When it starts to foam, reduce the heat to a slow rolling boil and add the Columbus hops. Add one fifth of the Cascade hops after 15 minutes, 30 minutes, 45 minutes, and 55 minutes. Prepare an ice bath by stopping the sink and filling it with 5 inches of water and ice. At the 60-minute mark, turn off the heat and add the remaining Cascade hops. Place the pot in the ice bath in the sink and cool to 70°F, about 30 minutes.

**FERMENT:** Using a sanitized funnel and strainer, pour the liquid into a sanitized fermenter. Add any water needed to fill the jug to the 1-gallon mark. Add the yeast, sanitize your hands, cover the mouth of the jug with one hand, and shake to distribute evenly. Attach a sanitized stopper and tubing to the fermenter and insert the other end of the tubing into a small bowl of sanitizing solution. The solution will begin to bubble as the yeast activates, pushing gas through the tube. Wait 2 to 3 days until the bubbling has slowed, then replace the tubing system with an airlock (see page 28). Wait 11 more days, then bottle, using the honey (see page 30 for bottling instructions).

## FOR 5 GALLONS

**60-minute mash at 152°F: 3¼ gallons water, plus 5 gallons for sparging; 9 pounds American 2-row malt, 2 pounds Caramel 20 malt, 1 pound Victory malt, 0.5 pound Munich malt**

**60-minute boil: 0.5 ounce Columbus hops; 2.5 ounces Cascade hops, divided into fifths**

**Ferment: 1 packet American ale yeast, such as Safale S-05 or Wyeast American Ale II; 1 cup honey, for bottling**

- - - - - - - - - - - - - - - -

## SUGGESTED FOOD PAIRINGS

- **Fried chicken**
- **Mac and cheese**
- **Bahn mi sandwiches**

# THESE TWO BEERS ARE GREAT ON THEIR OWN but are much better when poured together in the

classic Irish beer cocktail, the Black & Tan (known as "Half & Half" in Ireland). The "Black" is a super-dry Irish stout that has a creamy consistency. Flaked barley helps to approximate the super-smooth taste that Guinness gets from carbonating with nitrogen instead of carbon dioxide. The "Tan" is an ESB (extra-special bitter), a moderately hopped beer with a malty profile.

Serving Black & Tans is a great St. Patrick's Day party trick. When made correctly, the stout, which is lighter in alcohol and density, floats on top of the ESB. Pouring the stout over the tan is a delicate operation; go slow and steady. A special Black & Tan spoon that fits over a pint glass will help to slow the pour to a drip, giving you more control. If you don't have one, take an expendable metal spoon and bend back the stem to approximate the shape.

# BLACK & TAN BLACK 4.2% ABV

### 60-MINUTE MASH AT 152°F

1¾ quarts water, plus 1 gallon for
   sparging
1.0 pound Maris Otter malt
0.15 pound Chocolate malt
0.4 pound flaked barley
0.1 pound roasted barley
*all grains should be milled (see note,
 page 17)

### 60-MINUTE BOIL

0.15 ounce Challenger hops
0.4 ounce Fuggle hops,
   divided into halves

### FERMENT

½ packet English ale yeast,
   such as Nottingham (see
   note, page 22)
3 tablespoons maple syrup,
   for bottling

**MASH:** In a medium stockpot, heat the 1¾ quarts water over high heat to 160°F. Add all the malts and barleys and stir gently. The temperature should reduce to 150°F within 1 minute. Turn off the heat. Steep the grains for 60 minutes between 144°F and 152°F. Every 10 minutes, stir and take the temperature. If the grains get too cold, turn on the heat to high while stirring until the temperature rises to that range, then turn off the heat. With 10 minutes left, in a second medium stockpot heat the 1 gallon water to 170°F. After the grains have steeped for 60 minutes, raise the heat of the grains-and-water mixture to high and stir until the temperature reaches 170°F. Turn off the heat.

**SPARGE:** Place a fine-mesh strainer over a pot, and pour the grains into the strainer, reserving the liquid. Pour the 1 gallon of 170°F water over the grains. Recirculate the collected liquid through the grains once.

**BOIL:** Return the pot with the liquid to the stove on high heat and bring to a boil. When it starts to foam, reduce the heat to a slow rolling boil and add the Challenger hops. Add half of the Fuggle hops after 40 minutes and the remaining Fuggle hops after 50 minutes. Prepare an ice bath by stopping the sink and filling it with 5 inches of water and ice. At the 60-minute mark, turn off the heat. Place the pot in the ice bath in the sink and cool to 70°F, about 30 minutes.

**FERMENT:** Using a sanitized funnel and strainer, pour the liquid into a sanitized fermenter. Add any water needed to fill the jug to the 1-gallon mark. Add the yeast, sanitize your hands, cover the mouth of the jug with one hand, and shake to distribute evenly. Attach a sanitized stopper and tubing to the fermenter and insert the other end of the tubing into a small bowl of sanitizing solution. The solution will begin to bubble as the yeast activates, pushing gas through the tube. Wait 2 to 3 days until the bubbling has slowed, then replace the tubing system with an airlock (see page 28). Wait 11 more days, then bottle, using the maple syrup (see page 30 for bottling instructions).

**RECIPE CONTINUES**

## FOR 5 GALLONS

**60-minute mash at 152°F: 2 gallons water, plus 5 gallons for sparging; 5 pounds Maris Otter malt, 0.75 pound Chocolate malt, 2 pounds flaked barley, 0.5 pound roasted barley**

**60-minute boil: 0.75 ounce Challenger hops; 2 ounces Fuggle hops, divided into halves**

**Ferment: 1 packet English ale yeast, such as Nottingham; 1 cup maple syrup, for bottling**

# TAN 5.8% ABV

### 60-MINUTE MASH AT 152°F

2¼ quarts water, plus 1 gallon for sparging

1.75 pounds Golden Promise malt (or Maris Otter malt)

0.2 pound Victory malt

0.2 pound Caramel 40 malt

0.1 pound Caramel 20 malt

*all grains should be milled (see note, page 17)

### 60-MINUTE BOIL

0.15 ounce Challenger hops

0.2 ounce Whitbread Golding hops, divided into halves

### FERMENT

½ packet English ale yeast, such as Safale S-04 (see note, page 22)

3 tablespoons honey, for bottling

**MASH:** In a medium stockpot, heat the 2¼ quarts water over high heat to 160°F. Add all the malts and stir gently. The temperature should reduce to 150°F within 1 minute. Turn off the heat. Steep the grains for 60 minutes between 144°F and 152°F. Every 10 minutes, stir and take the temperature. If the grains get too cold, turn on the heat to high while stirring until the temperature rises to that range, then turn off the heat. With 10 minutes left, in a second medium stockpot heat the 1 gallon water to 170°F. After the grains have steeped for 60 minutes, raise the heat of the grains-and-water mixture to high and stir until the temperature reaches 170°F. Turn off the heat.

**SPARGE:** Place a fine-mesh strainer over a pot, and pour the grains into the strainer, reserving the liquid. Pour the 1 gallon of 170°F water over the grains. Recirculate the collected liquid through the grains once.

# POURING A BLACK & TAN

**BOIL:** Return the pot with the liquid to the stove on high heat and bring to a boil. When it starts to foam, reduce the heat to a slow rolling boil and add the Challenger hops. Add half of the Whitbread Golding hops after 30 minutes and the remaining Whitbread Golding hops after 55 minutes. Prepare an ice bath by stopping the sink and filling it with 5 inches of water and ice. At the 60-minute mark, turn off the heat. Place the pot in the ice bath in the sink and cool to 70°F, about 30 minutes.

**FERMENT:** Using a sanitized funnel and strainer, pour the liquid into a sanitized fermenter. Add any water needed to fill the jug to the 1-gallon mark. Add the yeast, sanitize your hands, cover the mouth of the jug with one hand, and shake to distribute evenly. Attach a sanitized stopper and tubing to the fermenter and insert the other end of the tubing into a small bowl of sanitizing solution. The solution will begin to bubble as the yeast activates, pushing gas through the tube. Wait 2 to 3 days until the bubbling has slowed, then replace the tubing system with an airlock (see page 28). Wait 11 more days, then bottle, using the honey (see page 30 for bottling instructions).

## FOR 5 GALLONS

**60-minute mash at 152°F: 3 gallons water, plus 5 gallons for sparging; 8.8 pounds Golden Promise malt, 1 pound Victory malt, 1 pound Caramel 40 malt, 0.5 pound Caramel 20 malt**

**60-minute boil: 0.75 ounce Challenger hops; 1 ounce Whitbread Golding hops, divided into halves**

**Ferment: 1 packet English ale yeast, such as Safale S-04; 1 cup honey, for bottling**

- - - - - - - - - - - - - - - -

## SUGGESTED FOOD PAIRINGS

- **Corned beef and cabbage**
- **Shepherd's pie**
- **Soda bread**

# THE LIGHT BODY AND SPICE OF A BELGIAN BLONDE ALE BASE makes the

perfect showcase for aromatic roses. We use a mix of ingredients to get the full rose profile: Rose hips (the dried fruit from the rose plant) add just a touch of fermentable sugar and reddish color, while the buds leave a heady floral aroma. A slightly sharper, almost apple-y Belgian ale yeast brings everything into focus.

# ROSE- 6.5% ABV
# CHEEKED
# & BLONDE

### 60-MINUTE MASH AT 152°F

2½ quarts water, plus 1 gallon for sparging

1.8 pounds Belgian Pilsner malt

0.4 pound Cara-pils malt

0.1 pound Aromatic malt

*all grains should be milled (see note, page 17)

### 60-MINUTE BOIL

0.25 ounce Styrian Golding hops, divided into fifths

1 teaspoon dried rose hips

1 tablespoon dried rosebuds

0.15 pound clear Belgian Candi Sugar (see note, page 22)

### FERMENT

½ packet Belgian ale yeast, such as Wyeast Belgian Strong (see note, page 22)

3 tablespoons honey, for bottling

**Note:** Our rose and lavender beers (see Lady Lavender, page 44) share the same grain base for a light-bodied Belgian blonde ale. We made them first as test batches, but then we couldn't choose between the two. Apparently, our customers feel the same way; whenever we serve them side by side, the tallies come back almost even. One happy solution is to make both. They're a perfect pair for brunch in the garden when everything has just started blooming.

**MASH:** In a medium stockpot, heat the 2½ quarts water over high heat to 160°F. Add all the malts and stir gently. The temperature should reduce to 150°F within 1 minute. Turn off the heat. Steep the grains for 60 minutes between 144°F and 152°F. Every 10 minutes, stir and take the temperature. If the grains get too cold, turn on the heat to high while stirring until the temperature rises to that range, then turn off the heat. With 10 minutes left, in a second medium stockpot heat the 1 gallon water to 170°F. After the grains have steeped for 60 minutes, raise the heat of the grains-and-water mixture to high and stir until the temperature reaches 170°F. Turn off the heat.

**SPARGE:** Place a fine-mesh strainer over a pot, and pour the grains into the strainer, reserving the liquid. Pour the 1 gallon of 170°F water over the grains. Recirculate the collected liquid through the grains once.

**BOIL:** Return the pot with the liquid to the stove on high heat and bring to a boil. When it starts to foam, reduce the heat to a slow rolling boil and add four fifths of the Styrian Golding hops. Add the rose hips after 20 minutes and the remaining hops after 55 minutes. Prepare an ice bath by stopping the sink and filling it with 5 inches of water and ice. At the 60-minute mark, turn off the heat, add the rosebuds and Belgian Candi Sugar, and stir to dissolve sugar. Place the pot in the ice bath in the sink and cool to 70°F, about 30 minutes.

**FERMENT:** Using a sanitized funnel and strainer, pour the liquid into a sanitized fermenter. Add any water needed to fill the jug to the 1-gallon mark. Add the yeast, sanitize your hands, cover the mouth of the jug with one hand, and shake to distribute evenly. Attach a sanitized stopper and tubing to the fermenter and insert the other end of the tubing into a small bowl of sanitizing solution. The solution will begin to bubble as the yeast activates, pushing gas through the tube. Wait 2 to 3 days until the bubbling has slowed, then replace the tubing system with an airlock (see page 28). Wait 11 more days, then bottle, using the honey (see page 30 for bottling instructions).

**Variation:** Instead of dried rosebuds, use fresh petals from 1 rose (about ¼ cup).

## FOR 5 GALLONS

**60-minute mash at 152°F: 3¼ gallons water, plus 5 gallons for sparging; 9 pounds Belgian Pilsner malt, 2 pounds Cara-pils malt, 0.5 pound Aromatic malt**

**60-minute boil: 1.25 ounces Styrian Golding hops, divided into fifths; 5 teaspoons dried rose hips; 5 tablespoons dried rosebuds; 0.75 pound clear Belgian Candi Sugar**

**Ferment: 1 packet Belgian ale yeast, such as Wyeast Belgian Strong; 1 cup honey, for bottling**

## SUGGESTED FOOD PAIRINGS

- **Spanakopita**
- **Quiches**
- **Donuts**

# THIS RECIPE IS BUILT FROM THE SAME BELGIAN BLONDE BASE AS THE ROSE-CHEEKED & BLONDE

(page 42), but it moves in an entirely different direction. The scent of lavender floats over the lightly spiced base and matches nicely with the hint of honey used for bottling. Stephen says that drinking it is like sitting on a swing in a field with your eyes closed.

# LADY LAVENDER
## 6.5% ABV

### 60-MINUTE MASH AT 152°F

2½ quarts water, plus 1 gallon for sparging

1.8 pounds Belgian Pilsner malt

0.4 pound Cara-pils malt

0.1 pound Aromatic malt

*all grains should be milled (see note, page 17)

### 60-MINUTE BOIL

0.25 ounce Styrian Golding hops, divided into fifths

4 teaspoons dried lavender flowers, divided into fourths

0.15 pound clear Belgian Candi Sugar (see note, page 22)

### FERMENT

½ packet Belgian ale yeast, such as Safale S-33 (see note, page 22)

3 tablespoons honey, for bottling

**MASH:** In a medium stockpot, heat the 2½ quarts water over high heat to 160°F. Add all the malts and stir gently. The temperature should reduce to 150°F within 1 minute. Turn off the heat. Steep the grains for 60 minutes between 144°F and 152°F. Every 10 minutes, stir and take the temperature. If the grains get too cold, turn on the heat to high while stirring until the temperature rises to that range, then turn off the heat. With 10 minutes left, in a second medium stockpot heat the 1 gallon water to 170°F. After the grains have steeped for 60 minutes, raise the heat of the grains-and-water mixture to high and stir until the temperature reaches 170°F. Turn off the heat.

**SPARGE:** Place a fine-mesh strainer over a pot, and pour the grains into the strainer, reserving the liquid. Pour the 1 gallon of 170°F water over the grains. Recirculate the collected liquid through the grains once.

**BOIL:** Return the pot with the liquid to the stove on high heat and bring to a boil. When it starts to foam, reduce the heat to a slow rolling boil and add four fifths of the Styrian Golding hops. Add 1 teaspoon of the lavender flowers after 30 minutes and the remaining hops after 55 minutes. Prepare an ice bath by stopping the sink and filling it with 5 inches of water and ice. At the 60-minute mark, turn off the heat, add the remaining lavender flowers and the Belgian Candi Sugar, and stir to dissolve the sugar. Place the pot in the ice bath in the sink and cool to 70°F, about 30 minutes.

**FERMENT:** Using a sanitized funnel and strainer, pour the liquid into a sanitized fermenter. Add any water needed to fill the jug to the 1-gallon mark. Add the yeast, sanitize your hands, cover the mouth of the jug with one hand, and shake to distribute evenly. Attach a sanitized stopper and tubing to the fermenter and insert the other end of the tubing into a small bowl of sanitizing solution. The solution will begin to bubble as the yeast activates, pushing gas through the tube. Wait 2 to 3 days until the bubbling has slowed, then replace the tubing system with an airlock (see page 28). Wait 11 more days, then bottle, using the honey (see page 30 for bottling instructions).

## FOR 5 GALLONS

**60-minute mash at 152°F: 3¼ gallons water, plus 5 gallons for sparging; 9 pounds Belgian Pilsner malt, 2 pounds Cara-pils malt, 0.5 pound Aromatic malt**

**60-minute boil: 1.25 ounces Styrian Golding hops, divided into fifths; ⅓ cup dried lavender flowers; 0.75 pound clear Belgian Candi Sugar**

**Ferment: 1 packet Belgian ale yeast, such as Safale S-33; 1 cup honey, for bottling**

- - - - - - - - - - - - - -

## SUGGESTED FOOD PAIRINGS

- **Grilled chicken**
- **Goat cheese**
- **Strawberry shortcake**

**FOR FATHER'S DAY,** branch out and get your dad something that you can make together (or at least drink together). Working at our Brooklyn Flea booth, we've helped steer many a befuddled gift giver to the right mix and have determined that most dads can be divided into light, brown, or dark beer drinkers. We created these three super-straightforward and dad-appropriate beers: a pale ale, a brown ale, and a stout.

# WORLD'S GREATEST DAD

## WGD **LIGHT** 5.0% ABV

This is a take on an American classic, the pale ale, featuring the citrusy Cascade hop flavor, a light body, and subtle fruitiness from the ale yeast.

### 60-MINUTE MASH AT 152°F

2 quarts water, plus 1 gallon for sparging

1.6 pounds American 2-row malt

0.1 pound Victory malt

0.1 pound Caramel 10 malt

0.1 pound Caramel 20 malt

*all grains should be milled (see note, page 17)

### 60-MINUTE BOIL

0.1 ounce Chinook hops

0.15 ounce Cascade hops, divided into thirds

### FERMENT

½ packet American ale yeast, such as Safale S-05 (see note, page 22)

3 tablespoons honey, for bottling

**MASH:** In a medium stockpot, heat the 2 quarts water over high heat to 160°F. Add all the malts and stir gently. The temperature should reduce to 150°F within 1 minute. Turn off the heat. Steep the grains for 60 minutes between 144°F and 152°F. Every 10 minutes, stir and take the temperature. If the grains get too cold, turn on the heat to high while stirring until the temperature rises to that range, then turn off the heat. With 10 minutes left, in a second medium stockpot heat the 1 gallon water to 170°F. After the grains have steeped for 60 minutes, raise the heat of the grains-and-water mixture to high and stir until the temperature reaches 170°F. Turn off the heat.

**SPARGE:** Place a fine-mesh strainer over a pot, and pour the grains into the strainer, reserving the liquid. Pour the 1 gallon of 170°F water over the grains. Recirculate the collected liquid through the grains once.

**BOIL:** Return the pot with the liquid to the stove on high heat and bring to a boil. When it starts to foam, reduce the heat to a slow rolling boil and add the Chinook hops. Add two thirds of the Cascade hops after 30 minutes and the remaining Cascade hops after 55 minutes. Prepare an ice bath by stopping the sink and filling it with 5 inches of water and ice. At the 60-minute mark, turn off the heat. Place the pot in the ice bath in the sink and cool to 70°F, about 30 minutes.

**FERMENT:** Using a sanitized funnel and strainer, pour the liquid into a sanitized fermenter. Add any water needed to fill the jug to the 1-gallon mark. Add the yeast, sanitize your hands, cover the mouth of the jug with one hand, and shake to distribute evenly. Attach a sanitized stopper and tubing to the fermenter and insert the other end of the tubing into a small bowl of sanitizing solution. The solution will begin to bubble as the yeast activates, pushing gas through the tube. Wait 2 to 3 days until the bubbling has slowed, then replace the tubing system with an airlock (see page 28). Wait 11 more days, then bottle, using the honey (see page 30 for bottling instructions).

**RECIPE CONTINUES**

## FOR 5 GALLONS

**60-minute mash at 152°F: 2½ gallons water, plus 5 gallons for sparging; 8 pounds American 2-row malt, 0.5 pound Victory malt, 0.5 pound Caramel 10 malt, 0.5 pound Caramel 20 malt**

**60-minute boil: 0.5 ounce Chinook hops; 0.75 ounce Cascade hops, divided into thirds**

**Ferment: 1 packet American ale yeast, such as Safale S-05; 1 cup honey, for bottling**

## SUGGESTED FOOD PAIRINGS

- **Hot dogs**
- **Corn on the cob**
- **Baked beans**

# WGD **BROWN** 5.0% ABV

A good easy-to-drink brown ale can be hard to come by. The moderate hop flavor, basic brown color, and nutty malty flavor don't seem difficult to achieve, but it's all about getting the right balance. Here we use traditional British ingredients to create just the right mix.

## 60-MINUTE MASH AT 152°F

- 2 quarts water, plus 1 gallon for sparging
- 1.6 pounds Maris Otter malt
- 0.1 pound Caramel 40 malt
- 0.1 pound Caramel 80 malt
- 0.1 pound Chocolate malt
- *all grains should be milled (see note, page 17)

## 60-MINUTE BOIL

- 0.1 ounce Challenger hops
- 0.15 ounce East Kent Golding hops, divided into thirds

## FERMENT

- ½ packet English ale yeast, such as Safale S-04 (see note, page 22)
- 3 tablespoons honey, for bottling

**MASH:** In a medium stockpot, heat the 2 quarts water over high heat to 160°F. Add all the malts and stir gently. The temperature should reduce to 150°F within 1 minute. Turn off the heat. Steep the grains for 60 minutes between 144°F and 152°F. Every 10 minutes, stir and take the temperature. If the grains get too cold, turn on the heat to high while stirring until the temperature rises to that range, then turn off the heat. With 10 minutes left, in a second medium stockpot heat the 1 gallon water to 170°F. After the grains have steeped for 60 minutes, raise the heat of the grains-and-water mixture to high and stir until the temperature reaches 170°F. Turn off the heat.

**SPARGE:** Place a fine-mesh strainer over a pot, and pour the grains into the strainer, reserving the liquid. Pour the 1 gallon of 170°F water over the grains. Recirculate the collected liquid through the grains once.

## FOR 5 GALLONS

**60-minute mash at 152°F: 2½ gallons water, plus 5 gallons for sparging; 8 pounds Maris Otter malt, 0.5 pound Caramel 40 malt, 0.5 pound Caramel 80 malt, 0.5 pound Chocolate malt**

**60-minute boil: 0.5 ounce Challenger hops; 0.75 ounce East Kent Golding hops, divided into thirds**

**Ferment: 1 packet English ale yeast, such as Safale S-04; 1 cup honey, for bottling**

**BOIL:** Return the pot with the liquid to the stove on high heat and bring to a boil. When it starts to foam, reduce the heat to a slow rolling boil and add the Challenger hops. Add two thirds of the East Kent Golding hops after 30 minutes and the remaining East Kent Golding hops after 55 minutes. Prepare an ice bath by stopping the sink and filling it with 5 inches of water and ice. At the 60-minute mark, turn off the heat. Place the pot in the ice bath in the sink and cool to 70°F, about 30 minutes.

**FERMENT:** Using a sanitized funnel and strainer, pour the liquid into a sanitized fermenter. Add any water needed to fill the jug to the 1-gallon mark. Add the yeast, sanitize your hands, cover the mouth of the jug with one hand, and shake to distribute evenly. Attach a sanitized stopper and tubing to the fermenter and insert the other end of the tubing into a small bowl of sanitizing solution. The solution will begin to bubble as the yeast activates, pushing gas through the tube. Wait 2 to 3 days until the bubbling has slowed, then replace the tubing system with an airlock (see page 28). Wait 11 more days, then bottle, using the honey (see page 30 for bottling instructions).

## SUGGESTED FOOD PAIRINGS
- **Fried fish**
- **Meat pies**
- **Pastrami sandwiches**

# WGD **DARK** 5.0% ABV

Dark, rich, malty stouts are one of the oldest styles of British beer. Lately, the fashion has leaned toward brewing extreme versions that spiral high in alcohol, but here's a solid recipe that's just the right amount of bitter, with a strong roasted character.

### 60-MINUTE MASH AT 152°F

2 quarts water, plus 1 gallon for sparging
1.5 pounds American 2-row malt
0.2 pound Caramel 40 malt
0.15 pound Chocolate malt
0.1 pound Caramel 120 malt
0.1 pound Black Patent malt
*all grains should be milled (see note, page 17)

### 60-MINUTE BOIL

0.15 ounce Northern Brewer hops
0.25 ounce Fuggle hops, divided into quarters

### FERMENT

½ packet English ale yeast, such as Nottingham (see note, page 22)
3 tablespoons maple syrup, for bottling

**RECIPE CONTINUES**

**MASH:** In a medium stockpot, heat the 2 quarts water over high heat to 160°F. Add all the malts and stir gently. The temperature should reduce to 150°F within 1 minute. Turn off the heat. Steep the grains for 60 minutes between 144°F and 152°F. Every 10 minutes, stir and take the temperature. If the grains get too cold, turn on the heat to high while stirring until the temperature rises to that range, then turn off the heat. With 10 minutes left, in a second medium stockpot heat the 1 gallon water to 170°F. After the grains have steeped for 60 minutes, raise the heat of the grains-and-water mixture to high and stir until the temperature reaches 170°F. Turn off the heat.

**SPARGE:** Place a fine-mesh strainer over a pot, and pour the grains into the strainer, reserving the liquid. Pour the 1 gallon of 170°F water over the grains. Recirculate the collected liquid through the grains once.

**BOIL:** Return the pot with the liquid to the stove on high heat and bring to a boil. When it starts to foam, reduce the heat to a slow rolling boil and add the Northern Brewer hops. Add three quarters of the Fuggle hops after 30 minutes and the remaining Fuggle hops after 50 minutes. Prepare an ice bath by stopping the sink and filling it with 5 inches of water and ice. At the 60-minute mark, turn off the heat. Place the pot in the ice bath in the sink and cool to 70°F, about 30 minutes.

**FERMENT:** Using a sanitized funnel and strainer, pour the liquid into a sanitized fermenter. Add any water needed to fill the jug to the 1-gallon mark. Add the yeast, sanitize your hands, cover the mouth of the jug with one hand, and shake to distribute evenly. Attach a sanitized stopper and tubing to the fermenter and insert the other end of the tubing into a small bowl of sanitizing solution. The solution will begin to bubble as the yeast activates, pushing gas through the tube. Wait 2 to 3 days until the bubbling has slowed, then replace the tubing system with an airlock (see page 28). Wait 11 more days, then bottle, using the maple syrup (see page 30 for bottling instructions).

## FOR 5 GALLONS

**60-minute mash at 152°F:** 2½ gallons water, plus 5 gallons for sparging; 7.5 pounds American 2-row malt, 1 pound Caramel 40 malt, 0.75 pound Chocolate malt, 0.5 pound Caramel 120 malt, 0.5 pound Black Patent malt

**60-minute boil:** 0.75 ounce Northern Brewer hops; 1.25 ounces Fuggle hops, divided into quarters

**Ferment:** 1 packet English ale yeast, such as Nottingham; 1 cup maple syrup, for bottling

- - - - - - - - - - - - - - - -

## SUGGESTED FOOD PAIRINGS

- **Oysters**
- **Chocolate cake**
- **Venison stew**

# WE FIRST CAME UPON A GOSE BEER,

a largely forgotten German style from Goslar, Germany, made with coriander and salt, while visiting Golden City Brewery in Colorado. It's light, sour, and the perfect palate cleanser for spring.

When we were asked to make a beer to pair with salt cod croquettes for a dinner party, we jumped at the chance to try our own take on gose. Mirroring the yuzu sauce in the dish (yuzu is a Japanese citrus that's similar to grapefruit, with a more concentrated flavor), we used a mix of lemon and lime peels in the beer. The trick: steeping some of the malt in a warm place for a couple of days to let the beer develop a slightly sour flavor.

# CITRUS GOSE 5.7% ABV

## PREP

1 cup water

0.2 pound German Pilsner malt for sour mash

1 lemon

1 lime

## 60-MINUTE MASH AT 152°F

2 quarts water, plus 1 gallon for sparging

1 pound German Pilsner malt

0.6 pound Pale Wheat malt

0.2 pound Munich malt

0.2 pound Acidulated malt

*all grains should be milled (see note, page 17)

## 60-MINUTE BOIL

0.4 ounce Tettnanger hops, divided into quarters

3 tablespoons coarse sea salt

3 tablespoons coriander seeds, crushed

## FERMENT

½ packet wheat ale yeast, such as Safbrew WB-06 (see note, page 22)

3 tablespoons honey, for bottling

**RECIPE CONTINUES**

**PREP:** Three days before brewing, heat 1 cup water in a small stockpot over high heat to 130°F. Turn off the heat, add the 0.2 pound of German Pilsner malt, and stir gently. The temperature should reduce to 120°F within 1 minute. Cover the pot and steep the grains for 45 minutes at 120°F. Every 10 minutes, stir and take the temperature. If the grains get too cold, turn on the heat to high while stirring until the temperature rises to 120°F. After 45 minutes, cover the surface of the grains with plastic wrap so no air touches the grains, and leave in a spot that reaches 115°F for 3 days, such as over a radiator or space heater or in a gas oven with only the pilot light on. This is how to make a "sour mash."

On the day of brewing, preheat the oven to 250°F. Peel the lemon and lime, reserving the peel. Place the pieces of the peel directly on a baking sheet and bake on the lower rack until they are dry, 10 to 15 minutes, or until the peels begin to brown.

**MASH:** In a medium stockpot, heat the 2 quarts water over high heat to 160°F. Add all the malts and stir gently. The temperature should reduce to 150°F within 1 minute. Turn off the heat. Steep the grains for 60 minutes between 144°F and 152°F. Every 10 minutes, stir and take the temperature. If the grains get too cold, turn on the heat to high while stirring until the temperature rises to that range, then turn off the heat. With 10 minutes left, in a second medium stockpot heat the 1 gallon water to 170°F. After the grains have steeped for 60 minutes, raise the heat of the grains-and-water mixture to high and stir until the temperature reaches 170°F. Turn off the heat.

**SPARGE:** Place a fine-mesh strainer over a pot, and pour the grains (including those from the sour mash) into the strainer, reserving the liquid. Pour the 1 gallon of 170°F water over the grains. Recirculate the collected liquid through the grains once.

**BOIL:** Return the pot with the liquid to the stove on high heat and bring to a boil. When it starts to foam, reduce the heat to a slow rolling boil. Add half of the Tettnanger hops after 15 minutes, one quarter of the hops after 30 minutes, the remaining hops after 45 minutes, and the lemon and lime peels after 55 minutes. Prepare an ice bath by stopping the sink and filling it with 5 inches of water and ice. At the 60-minute mark, turn off the heat and add the sea salt and coriander. Stir to dissolve salt using a sanitized spoon. Place the pot in the ice bath in the sink and cool to 70°F, about 30 minutes.

**FERMENT:** Using a sanitized funnel and strainer, pour the liquid into a sanitized fermenter. Add any water needed to fill the jug to the 1-gallon mark. Add the yeast, sanitize your hands, cover the mouth of the jug with one hand, and shake to distribute evenly. Attach a sanitized stopper and tubing to the fermenter and insert the other end of the tubing into a small bowl of sanitizing solution. The solution will begin to bubble as the yeast activates, pushing gas through the tube. Wait 2 to 3 days until the bubbling has slowed, then replace the tubing system with an airlock (see page 28). Wait 11 more days, then bottle, using the honey (see page 30 for bottling instructions).

## GOSE BOTTLES

A gose bottle traditionally has a really long neck without a cap. The active yeast inside the beer swells up and clogs the bottle's opening, creating a natural cork. Pretty gross if you think about it for too long, but tart and delicious if you drink it instead.

## FOR 5 GALLONS

**Prep: 1 pound German Pilsner malt for sour mash, 5 cups water, 5 lemons, 5 limes**

**60-minute mash at 152°F: 2½ gallons water, plus 5 gallons for sparging; 5 pounds German Pilsner malt, 3 pounds Pale Wheat malt, 1 pound Munich malt, 1 pound Acidulated malt**

**60-minute boil: 2 ounces Tettnanger hops, divided into quarters; 1 cup sea salt; 1 cup coriander seeds, crushed**

**Ferment: 1 packet wheat ale yeast, such as Safbrew WB-06; 1 cup honey, for bottling**

- - - - - - - - - - - - - - - - -

## SUGGESTED FOOD PAIRINGS

· **Salted fish**
· **Smoked seafood**
· **Croquettes**

**TANNIC, AROMATIC BLACK TEA IS THE PERFECT PARTNER FOR BEER. ASSAM TEA,** a variety from the north of India, is prized for its malted barley-like flavor. Earl Grey has a citrusy component that complements beer well. We've seen it done with chai blends, Darjeeling, and green jasmine, too. Here we use English Breakfast, but you can use any variety that you like. We built a base made from special biscuit malt that has been roasted to taste like toasted bread, hence the "tea-and-toast" moniker. The result is a bready, sophisticated pint—the perfect grown-up afternoon drink for the ladies (and gentlemen) who lunch.

# TEA & TOAST 5.6% ABV

### 60-MINUTE MASH AT 152°F

2¼ quarts water, plus 1 gallon for sparging

1.5 pounds Belgian Pilsner malt

0.3 pound Biscuit malt

0.2 pound Caramel 10 malt

0.1 pound Munich malt

0.1 pound torrified wheat

*all grains should be milled (see note, page 17)

### 60-MINUTE BOIL

0.1 ounce Styrian Golding hops

0.2 ounce Saaz hops, divided into halves

3 teaspoons loose English Breakfast tea (or 1 tea bag)

### FERMENT

½ packet Belgian ale yeast, such as Safale S-33 (see note, page 22)

3 tablespoons honey, for bottling

**Note:** Just as with regular tea, the longer you let the tea steep, the more astringent and bitter your beer will be. When using black tea, we recommend three to five minutes for a balanced brew.

**MASH:** In a medium stockpot, heat the 2¼ quarts water over high heat to 160°F. Add all the malts and torrified wheat and stir gently. The temperature should reduce to 150°F within 1 minute. Turn off the heat. Steep the malts and the wheat for 60 minutes between 144°F and 152°F. Every 10 minutes, stir and take the temperature. If the grains get too cold, turn on the heat to high while stirring until the temperature rises to that range, then turn off the heat. With 10 minutes left, in a second medium stockpot heat the 1 gallon water to 170°F. After the grains have steeped for 60 minutes, raise the heat of the grains-and-water mixture to high and stir until the temperature reaches 170°F. Turn off the heat.

**SPARGE:** Place a fine-mesh strainer over a pot, and pour the grains into the strainer, reserving the liquid. Pour the 1 gallon of 170°F water over the grains. Recirculate the collected liquid through the grains once.

**BOIL:** Return the pot with the liquid to the stove on high heat and bring to a boil. When it starts to foam, reduce the heat to a slow rolling boil and add the Styrian Golding hops. Add half of the Saaz hops after 30 minutes and the remaining Saaz hops after 45 minutes. Prepare an ice bath by stopping the sink and filling it with 5 inches of water and ice. At the 60-minute mark, turn off the heat and add the tea. Place the pot in the ice bath in the sink and cool to 70°F, about 30 minutes. Take out the tea after 5 minutes (see note).

**FERMENT:** Using a sanitized funnel and strainer, pour the liquid into a sanitized fermenter. Add any water needed to fill the jug to the 1-gallon mark. Add the yeast, sanitize your hands, cover the mouth of the jug with one hand, and shake to distribute evenly. Attach a sanitized stopper and tubing to the fermenter and insert the other end of the tubing into a small bowl of sanitizing solution. The solution will begin to bubble as the yeast activates, pushing gas through the tube. Wait 2 to 3 days until the bubbling has slowed, then replace the tubing system with an airlock (see page 28). Wait 11 more days, then bottle, using the honey (see page 30 for bottling instructions).

## FOR 5 GALLONS

**60-minute mash at 152°F: 2¾ gallons water, plus 5 gallons for sparging; 7.5 pounds Belgian Pilsner malt, 1.5 pounds Biscuit malt, 1 pound Caramel 10 malt, 0.5 pound Munich malt, 0.5 pound torrified wheat**

**60-minute boil: 0.5 ounce Styrian Golding hops; 1 ounce Saaz hops, divided into halves; ⅓ cup loose English Breakfast tea (or 5 bags)**

**Ferment: 1 packet Belgian ale yeast, such as Safale S-33; 1 cup honey, for bottling**

## SUGGESTED FOOD PAIRINGS

- **Savory scones**
- **Fish in cream sauce**
- **Egg dishes**

# WE DON'T MAKE MANY LAGERS BECAUSE THE SPECIAL YEASTS

need much cooler temperatures to create that classic crisp taste. California Commons, a style that originated on the West Coast in the nineteenth century, is the result of fermenting a lager at room temperature. Our Spring Lager is a fairly straightforward take on the style: mildly fruity, amber in color, and deftly hopped.

# SPRING LAGER

## 5.1% ABV

### 60-MINUTE MASH AT 152°F

2 quarts water, plus 1 gallon for sparging

1.6 pound Pale Ale malt

0.2 pound Caramel 10 malt

0.2 pound Caramel 40 malt

*all grains should be milled (see note, page 17)

### 60-MINUTE BOIL

0.6 ounce Northern Brewer hops, divided into sixths

### FERMENT

½ packet lager yeast, such as Saflager S-23 (see note, page 22)

3 tablespoons honey, for bottling

**MASH:** In a medium stockpot, heat the 2 quarts water over high heat to 160°F. Add all the malts and stir gently. The temperature should reduce to 150°F within 1 minute. Turn off the heat. Steep the grains for 60 minutes between 144°F and 152°F. Every 10 minutes, stir and take the temperature. If the grains get too cold, turn on the heat to high while stirring until the temperature rises to that range, then turn off the heat. With 10 minutes left, in a second medium stockpot heat the 1 gallon water to 170°F. After the grains have steeped for 60 minutes, raise the heat of the grains-and-water mixture to high and stir until the temperature reaches 170°F. Turn off the heat.

**SPARGE:** Place a fine-mesh strainer over a pot, and pour the grains into the strainer, reserving the liquid. Pour the 1 gallon of 170°F water over the grains. Recirculate the collected liquid through the grains once.

**BOIL:** Return the pot with the liquid to the stove on high heat and bring to a boil. When it starts to foam, reduce the heat to a slow rolling boil and add one sixth of the Northern Brewer hops. Add another sixth of the hops after 15 minutes, 30 minutes, 45 minutes, and 55 minutes. Prepare an ice bath by stopping the sink and filling it with 5 inches of water and ice. At the 60-minute mark, turn off the heat and add the remaining hops. Place the pot in the ice bath in the sink and cool to 70°F, about 30 minutes.

**FERMENT:** Using a sanitized funnel and strainer, pour the liquid into a sanitized fermenter. Add any water needed to fill the jug to the 1-gallon mark. Add the yeast, sanitize your hands, cover the mouth of the jug with one hand, and shake to distribute evenly. Attach a sanitized stopper and tubing to the fermenter and insert the other end of the tubing into a small bowl of sanitizing solution. The solution will begin to bubble as the yeast activates, pushing gas through the tube. Wait 2 to 3 days until the bubbling has slowed, then replace the tubing system with an airlock (see page 28). Wait 11 more days, then bottle, using the honey (see page 30 for bottling instructions).

## FOR 5 GALLONS

**60-minute mash at 152°F: 2½ gallons water, plus 5 gallons for sparging; 8 pounds Pale Ale malt, 1 pound Caramel 10 malt, 1 pound Caramel 40 malt**

**60-minute boil: 3 ounces Northern Brewer hops, divided into sixths**

**Ferment: 1 packet lager yeast, such as Saflager S-23; 1 cup honey, for bottling**

- - - - - - - - - - - - - - -

## SUGGESTED FOOD PAIRINGS

· **Mushrooms**
· **Mild cheese**
· **Green vegetables**

# THIS IS OUR TAKE ON EDELWEISS,

the somewhat obscure German style of hefeweizen, a cloudy wheat beer. It gets bottled early, just a few days after adding the yeast and without any extra honey or syrup. The beer finishes fermenting in the bottle and gathers a light carbonation. The result is a floral, yeasty beer that ends up on the sweeter side of the wheat beer spectrum—more bubble gum and banana than spicy clove. This beer is soft and gentle, making it ideal for springtime.

# EDELWEISS
## 5.0% ABV

### 60-MINUTE MASH AT 152°F

2 quarts water, plus 1 gallon for sparging

1 pound Pale Wheat malt

0.5 pound German Pilsner malt

0.4 pound Munich malt

0.08 pound Melanoidin malt

*all grains should be milled (see note, page 17)

### 60-MINUTE BOIL

0.08 ounce Centennial hops, divided into halves

0.04 ounce Amarillo hops

### FERMENT

½ packet wheat ale yeast, such as White Labs Hefeweizen Ale (see note, page 22)

**MASH:** In a medium stockpot, heat the 2 quarts water over high heat to 160°F. Add all the malts and stir gently. The temperature should reduce to 150°F within 1 minute. Turn off the heat. Steep the grains for 60 minutes between 144°F and 152°F. Every 10 minutes, stir and take the temperature. If the grains get too cold, turn on the heat to high while stirring until the temperature rises to that range, then turn off the heat. With 10 minutes left, in a second medium stockpot heat the 1 gallon water to 170°F. After the grains have steeped for 60 minutes, raise the heat of the grains-and-water mixture to high and stir until the temperature reaches 170°F. Turn off the heat.

**SPARGE:** Place a fine-mesh strainer over a pot, and pour the grains into the strainer, reserving the liquid. Pour the 1 gallon of 170°F water over the grains. Recirculate the collected liquid through the grains once.

**BOIL:** Return the pot with the liquid to the stove on high heat and bring to a boil. When it starts to foam, reduce the heat to a slow rolling boil and add half of the Centennial hops. Add the remaining Centennial hops after 30 minutes and the Amarillo hops after 58 minutes. Prepare an ice bath by stopping the sink and filling it with 5 inches of water and ice. At the 60-minute mark, turn off the heat. Place the pot in the ice bath in the sink and cool to 70°F, about 30 minutes.

**FERMENT:** Using a sanitized funnel and strainer, pour the liquid into a sanitized fermenter. Add any water needed to fill the jug to the 1-gallon mark. Add the yeast, sanitize your hands, cover the mouth of the jug with one hand, and shake to distribute evenly. Attach a sanitized stopper and tubing to the fermenter and insert the other end of the tubing into a small bowl of sanitizing solution. The solution will begin to bubble as the yeast activates, pushing gas through the tube. Wait 3 days, then bottle (see page 30 for bottling instructions). No bottling sugar is needed; the beer will carbonate on its own.

## FOR 5 GALLONS

**60-minute mash at 152°F: 2½ gallons water, plus 5 gallons for sparging; 5 pounds Pale Wheat malt, 2.5 pounds German Pilsner malt, 2 pounds Munich malt, 0.5 pound Melanoidin malt**

**60-minute boil: 0.5 ounce Centennial hops, divided into halves; 0.25 ounce Amarillo hops**

**Ferment: 1 packet wheat ale yeast, such as White Labs Hefeweizen Ale**

- - - - - - - - - - - - - - -

## SUGGESTED FOOD PAIRINGS

- **Spicy curries**
- **Fried chicken**
- **Mexican food**

**WE WILL ADMIT IT:** We were skeptical of gluten-free beers. The commercial versions usually use sorghum syrup, which can be thin, watery, and sour. But with so many requests from customers with a gluten intolerance, we decided to see if we could come up with something better. By using what we learned while making the Pumpkin Dubbel (page 124)—that fermentable sugars could come from root vegetables, too, not just grain—we hit on a recipe using carrots that worked so well we even fooled our staff into thinking it was "real beer." It's light, hoppy, and refreshing, and it tastes a lot like beer made with barley. Although it's light in color, it's not actually a pilsner. The name is a beer-nerd joke: "Cara-pils" is a specialty grain.

This beer is hopped pretty aggressively—almost like an I.P.A. The extra flavor helps compensate for the absent maltiness.

# GLUTEN-FREE CARROT-PILS 3.5% ABV

## 60-MINUTE MASH AT 152°F

- 2½ quarts water, plus 1 gallon for sparging
- 1 pound carrots, peeled and grated
- 0.5 pound uncooked basmati rice
- 1 pound uncooked red quinoa
- 0.2 pound rice hulls (see note)

## 60-MINUTE BOIL

- 0.1 ounce Columbus hops
- 0.5 ounce Cascade hops, divided into fifths
- 1 cup sugar

## FERMENT

- ½ packet gluten-free ale yeast, such as Nottingham (see note, page 22)
- 3 tablespoons honey, for bottling

**Note:** Rice hulls help filter the mash, but you may still need to give the wet grains a squeeze during sparging to extract all the sugar.

**MASH:** In a medium stockpot, heat the 2½ quarts water over high heat to 160°F. Add the carrots, rice, quinoa, and rice hulls and stir gently. The temperature should reduce to 150°F within 1 minute. Turn off the heat. Steep the carrots and grains for 60 minutes between 144°F and 152°F. Every 10 minutes, stir and take the temperature. If the carrots and grains get too cold, turn on the heat to high while stirring until the temperature rises to that range, then turn off the heat. With 10 minutes left, in a second medium stockpot heat 1 gallon water to 170°F. After the carrots and grains have steeped for 60 minutes, raise the heat of the carrots-grains mixture to high and stir until the temperature reaches 170°F. Turn off the heat.

**SPARGE:** Place a fine-mesh strainer over a pot and pour the carrots and grains into the strainer, reserving the liquid. Use a large spoon to press all the liquid out of the strainer. Pour the 1 gallon of 170°F water over the carrots and grains. Recirculate the collected liquid through the grains and carrots once.

**BOIL:** Return the pot with the liquid to the stove on high heat and bring to a boil. When it starts to foam, reduce the heat to a slow rolling boil and add the Columbus hops. Add one fifth of the Cascade hops after 15 minutes, 30 minutes, 45 minutes, and 55 minutes. Prepare an ice bath by stopping the sink and filling it with 5 inches of water and ice. At the 60-minute mark, turn off the heat, add the remaining Cascade hops and the sugar, and stir to dissolve the sugar. Place the pot in the ice bath in the sink and cool to 70°F, about 30 minutes.

**FERMENT:** Using a sanitized funnel and strainer, pour the liquid into a sanitized fermenter. Add any water needed to fill the jug to the 1-gallon mark. Add the gluten-free yeast, sanitize your hands, cover the mouth of the jug with one hand, and shake to distribute evenly. Attach a sanitized stopper and tubing to the fermenter and insert the other end of the tubing into a small bowl of sanitizing solution. The solution will begin to bubble as the yeast activates, pushing gas through the tube. Wait 2 to 3 days until the bubbling has slowed, then replace the tubing system with an airlock (see page 28). Wait 11 more days, then bottle, using the honey (see page 30 for bottling instructions).

## FOR 5 GALLONS

**60-minute mash at 152°F: 3 gallons water, plus 5 gallons for sparging; 5 pounds carrots, peeled and grated; 2.5 pounds uncooked basmati rice; 5 pounds uncooked red quinoa; 0.5 pound rice hulls**

**60-minute boil: 0.5 ounce Columbus hops; 2.5 ounces Cascade hops, divided into fifths; 5 cups sugar**

**Ferment: 1 packet gluten-free ale yeast, such as Nottingham; 1 cup honey, for bottling**

- - - - - - - - - - - - - -

## SUGGESTED FOOD PAIRINGS

- **Potato salad**
- **Coleslaw**
- **Grilled chicken**

# BEER-BATTERED
# FRIED VEGETABLES

Beer batters are the best for frying. Alcohol evaporates at a quicker rate than water does and the foam helps to insulate the veggies, so they stay crisp in the hot oil instead of soaking it up. Almost all vegetables work here; use the ones you like most. We love asparagus and green beans.

**SERVES 4 to 6 as an appetizer**

1 cup all-purpose flour

1 teaspoon salt, plus more to taste

1 tablespoon grated lime zest

⅓ teaspoon freshly ground black pepper

¼ teaspoon cayenne pepper

1 cup light beer, such as World's Greatest Dad Light (page 46), Tan (page 40), or Spring Lager (page 56)

Peanut or vegetable oil, for frying

3 cups vegetables (such as asparagus and green beans), trimmed roughly to the same size of ½-inch × 4-inch stick

- - - - - - - - - - - - - - - - - - - - - - - - - - - - - - - - - - - - - - - - - - -

In a large bowl, whisk together the flour, salt, lime zest, black pepper, and cayenne pepper. While continuing to whisk, slowly pour the beer into the flour mixture and beat until smooth. Let the mixture sit for 1 hour at room temperature.

Heat 4 inches of oil in a 3- to 4-quart heavy saucepan over high heat until the temperature rises to 375°F, using a deep-frying thermometer. Line a plate with paper towels. One at a time, dunk the vegetables in the batter to coat, then shake off the excess batter and place the vegetables in the hot oil using long-handled tongs. Agitate the oil with a spoon if necessary to prevent the vegetables from sticking together. Fry the vegetables until the batter turns golden brown, 2 to 3 minutes, then, with a slotted spoon, transfer them to the paper-lined plate. Sprinkle with salt to taste. Serve warm.

# LAVENDER SHORTBREAD WITH HONEY-BEER GLAZE

Lavender adds a savory counterpoint to these sweet, sticky cookies. The honey and beer in the glaze echo the ingredients in our Lady Lavender beer. They make great gifts, if you don't eat them all first.

**MAKES 24 cookies**

## FOR THE SHORTBREAD

½ pound (2 sticks) unsalted butter, cut into little pieces and chilled

⅔ cup packed dark brown sugar

Pinch of salt

2 cups unbleached all-purpose flour

2 tablespoons finely chopped dried lavender

## FOR THE HONEY-BEER GLAZE

½ cup granulated sugar

½ cup honey

½ cup light beer, such as Lady Lavender (page 44)

1 tablespoon fresh lemon juice

---

**FOR THE SHORTBREAD:** Preheat the oven to 350°F. With a food processor or by hand, beat the butter, brown sugar, and salt until creamy. Gently stir in the flour and lavender until just combined. Press the mixture into an even layer in the bottom of a 9-inch pie pan. Prick the top of the dough all over with a fork. Bake for 25 minutes in the oven, or until the edges are golden brown. Remove from the oven and let the shortbread rest for 10 minutes, then cut into wedges and let cool in the pan.

**FOR THE GLAZE:** In a small saucepan, bring the granulated sugar, honey, beer, and lemon juice to a boil over medium-high heat, stirring constantly with a metal spoon to dissolve the sugar. Turn the heat to medium-low and simmer until the mixture has been reduced to a syrupy consistency, about 10 minutes. Let cool. Brush the glaze onto the shortbread wedges and chill them in the fridge to set the glaze.

# SUMMER

**PERHAPS IF WE LIVED IN CALIFORNIA WHERE THE GROWING SEASON STRETCHES NEARLY TWICE AS LONG,** we'd be more casual about summer produce. But come June, when the berries start showing up in markets, the race is on to put them in everything—cereal, salads, desserts, and, yes, beer. It helps that fruit and beer are a great match. Berries and stone fruits have plenty of fermentable sugar, and they can complement the already fruity taste of some malts.

In summer, you want your drinks to be fun and refreshing—a beer (or two) that goes with that trashy detective novel you bought for reading at the beach or the midnight screening of a surfing movie that you've projected onto a sheet in the backyard. We make large batches of smoked beer for barbecues in the park or roof parties that stretch from sunset until the wee hours. Small batches are for camping, clambakes, or hanging out on our stoop with friends.

GRAPEFRUIT HONEY ALE

---

BBQ BEER

---

BLACKBERRY RED ALE

---

SIMCOE I.P.A.

---

JALAPEÑO SAISON MILD

---

JALAPEÑO SAISON SPICY

---

SMOKED CHERRY

---

S'MORE BEER

---

LOBSTER SAISON

---

PEACH COBBLER ALE

---

BEL-GIN STRONG

---

KÖLSCH

---

GLUTEN-FREE BEET-BUCKWHEAT ALE

---

BBQ BEER BARBECUE SAUCE

---

BEL-GIN STRONG BEER-BRINED PICKLES

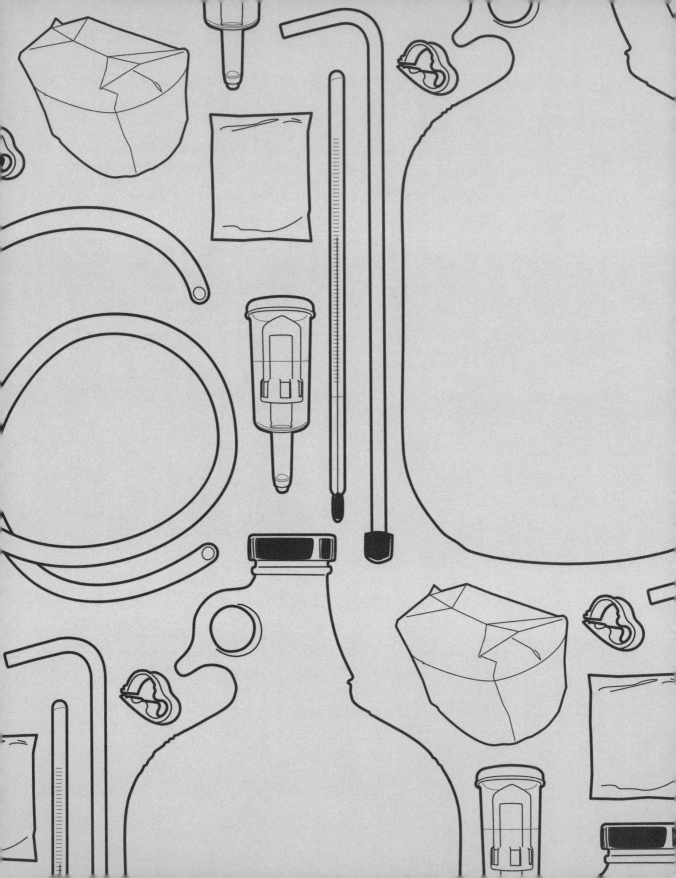

# SUMMER FEATURE
# BREWING BEER IN THE HEAT OF SUMMER

If you brew beer for long enough, someone will most likely tell you that ale yeast needs to ferment at temperatures from 60°F to 75°F. Actually, that's the range in which ale yeast is happiest. Entire styles of brewing were built upon brewing in hot summer weather; certain saisons, for example, use strains of yeasts that work best at 90°F.

Our summer recipes are optimal for hot-weather brewing. Yeasts work faster in warmer temperatures and often leave you with fruitier-tasting beers, as the yeasts produce more esters—aromatic molecules—at the higher temps. We've never had air-conditioning in any apartment we've brewed in, but that hasn't stopped us from having great beer on tap year-round.

If the temperature of your apartment or home is really spiking (over 90°F), wrap the fermenter in a wet towel. Brewing supply stores carry something called a carboy coat, if you want to invest in that, but it's not super-necessary. If you're looking at the thermostat and getting nervous, just remember that liquids take a lot more energy to heat up and cool down than air does, so your beer won't be affected as quickly by the ambient temperature swings in a room.

# THIS REFRESHING LIGHT-BODIED PALE ALE IS ONE OF OUR BEST SELLERS.

Hops and grapefruit are a natural pair: They are both bitter, and many hops—especially American varieties—have citrusy profiles. For this recipe, we chose Amarillo hops from Washington State because they have a particularly grapefruity aroma. A touch of honey in the boil mellows the bitterness and provides a smooth finish. The final result is a crisp beer that appeals to all palates. It even won over Erica's non-beer-drinking mom.

# GRAPEFRUIT
# HONEY ALE 5.5% ABV

## PREP

Peel from 1 scrubbed and dried grapefruit

## 60-MINUTE MASH AT 152°F

2 quarts water, plus 1 gallon for sparging

1.35 pounds English Pale malt

0.1 pound Victory malt

0.1 pound Caramel 10 malt

0.1 pound Caramel 20 malt

0.15 pound torrified wheat

*all grains should be milled (see note, page 17)

## 60-MINUTE BOIL

0.1 ounce Columbus hops

0.2 ounce Amarillo hops, divided into halves

0.2 pound clear Belgian Candi Sugar (see note, page 22)

¼ cup honey

## FERMENT

½ packet English ale yeast, such as Safale S-04 (see note, page 22)

3 tablespoons honey, for bottling

**PREP:** Preheat the oven to 250°F. Place the pieces of grapefruit peel directly on a baking sheet and bake on the lower rack until they are dry, 15 to 20 minutes, or until the peel begins to brown.

**MASH:** In a medium stockpot, heat the 2 quarts water over high heat to 160°F. Add all the malts and torrified wheat and stir gently. The temperature should reduce to 150°F within 1 minute. Turn off the heat. Steep the grains for 60 minutes between 144°F and 152°F. Every

10 minutes, stir and take the temperature. If the grains get too cold, turn on the heat to high while stirring until the temperature rises to that range, then turn off the heat. With 10 minutes left, in a second medium stockpot heat the 1 gallon water to 170°F. After the grains have steeped for 60 minutes, raise the heat of the grains-and-water mixture to high and stir until the temperature reaches 170°F. Turn off the heat.

**SPARGE:** Place a fine-mesh strainer over a pot, and pour the grains into the strainer, reserving the liquid. Pour the 1 gallon of 170°F water over the grains. Recirculate the collected liquid through the grain once.

**BOIL:** Return the pot with the liquid to the stove on high heat and bring to a boil. When it starts to foam, reduce the heat to a slow rolling boil and add the Columbus hops. Add half of the Amarillo hops after 30 minutes, the grapefruit peel after 55 minutes, and the remaining Amarillo hops after 59 minutes. Prepare an ice bath by stopping the sink and filling it with 5 inches of water and ice. At the 60-minute mark, turn off the heat, add the Belgian Candi Sugar and ¼ cup honey, and stir to dissolve. Place the pot in the ice bath in the sink and cool to 70°F, about 30 minutes.

**FERMENT:** Using a sanitized funnel and strainer, pour the liquid into a sanitized fermenter. Add any water needed to fill the jug to the 1-gallon mark. Add the yeast, sanitize your hands, cover the mouth of the jug with one hand, and shake to distribute evenly. Attach a sanitized stopper and tubing to the fermenter and insert the other end of the tubing into a small bowl of sanitizing solution. The solution will begin to bubble as the yeast activates, pushing gas through the tube. Wait 2 to 3 days until the bubbling has slowed, then replace the tubing system with an airlock (see page 28). Wait 11 more days, then bottle, using the 3 tablespoons honey (see page 30 for bottling instructions).

**Variations:** Noah, a frequent customer who manned the McClure's pickle booth at the Brooklyn Flea, stopped by our tent with a bottle of beer he had made using this recipe, only he had substituted ginger for the grapefruit. We loved it. You'll need about 1½ tablespoons of fresh grated ginger. Add it at 55 minutes into the boil.

Agave nectar will work as a substitution for honey.

## FOR 5 GALLONS

**Prep: Peel from 5 grapefruits**

**60-minute mash at 152°F: 2½ gallons water, plus 5 gallons for sparging; 6.75 pounds English Pale malt, 0.5 pound Victory malt, 0.5 pound Caramel 10 malt, 0.5 pound Caramel 20 malt; 0.75 pound torrified wheat**

**60-minute boil: 0.5 ounce Columbus hops; 1 ounce Amarillo hops, divided into halves; 1 pound clear Belgian Candi Sugar; 1¼ cups honey, plus 1 cup for bottling**

**Ferment: 1 packet English ale yeast, such as Safale S-04**

- - - - - - - - - - - - - -

## SUGGESTED FOOD PAIRINGS

- **Roasted chicken**
- **Poached fish**
- **Goat cheese**

- - - - - - - - - - - - - -

**Note:** Hops, like other crops, experience shortages depending on the growing season. Amarillo stocks can vary from year to year. So if you have a hard time finding them, try Centennial or Cascade for a citrus-filled hop character.

# THIS SMOKED BEER IS BASED ON RAUCHBIER, a traditional style made in Bamberg, Germany.

Most barley malts are roasted in a closed kiln, but some of the malt in this beer is smoked over beechwood, which gives a deep, smoky, almost bacon-like flavor. The resulting beer is light and refreshing and complements anything off the barbecue.

# BBQ BEER 5.5% ABV

## 60-MINUTE MASH AT 152°F

2¼ quarts water, plus 1 gallon for sparging

0.8 pound Smoked malt

0.7 pound German Pilsner malt

0.4 pound Munich malt

0.25 pound Caramunich malt

0.1 pound Cara-pils malt

*all grains should be milled (see note, page 17)

## 60-MINUTE BOIL

0.25 ounce Tettnanger hops, divided into halves

0.3 ounce Hallertau hops, divided into thirds

## FERMENT

½ packet American ale yeast, such as Safale S-05 (see note, page 22)

3 tablespoons maple syrup, for bottling

**MASH:** In a medium stockpot, heat the 2¼ quarts water over high heat to 160°F. Add all the malts and stir gently. The temperature should reduce to 150°F within 1 minute. Turn off the heat. Steep the grains for 60 minutes between 144°F and 152°F. Every 10 minutes, stir and take the temperature. If the grains get too cold, turn on the heat to high while stirring until the temperature rises to that range, then turn off the heat. With 10 minutes left, in a second medium stockpot heat the 1 gallon water to 170°F. After the grains have steeped for 60 minutes, raise the heat of the grains-and-water mixture to high and stir until the temperature reaches 170°F. Turn off the heat.

**SPARGE:** Place a fine-mesh strainer over a pot, and pour the grains into the strainer, reserving the liquid. Pour the 1 gallon of 170°F water over the grains. Recirculate the collected liquid through the grains once.

**BOIL:** Return the pot with the liquid to the stove on high heat and bring to a boil. When it starts to foam, reduce the heat to a slow rolling boil and add half of the Tettnanger hops. Add the remaining Tettnanger hops after 30 minutes and one third of the Hallertau hops after 45 minutes and another third after 55 minutes. Prepare an ice bath by stopping the sink and filling it with 5 inches of water and ice. At the 60-minute mark, turn off the heat and add the remaining Hallertau hops. Place the pot in the ice bath in the sink and cool to 70°F, about 30 minutes.

**FERMENT:** Using a sanitized funnel and strainer, pour the liquid into a sanitized fermenter. Add any water needed to fill the jug to the 1-gallon mark. Add the yeast, sanitize your hands, cover the mouth of the jug with one hand, and shake to distribute evenly. Attach a sanitized stopper and tubing to the fermenter and insert the other end of the tubing into a small bowl of sanitizing solution. The solution will begin to bubble as the yeast activates, pushing gas through the tube. Wait 2 to 3 days until the bubbling has slowed, then replace the tubing system with an airlock (see page 28). Wait 11 more days, then bottle, using the maple syrup (see page 30 for bottling instructions).

## FOR 5 GALLONS

**60-minute mash at 152°F: 3 gallons water, plus 5 gallons for sparging; 4 pounds Smoked malt, 3.5 pounds German Pilsner malt, 2 pounds Munich malt, 1.25 pounds Caramunich malt, 0.5 pound Cara-pils malt**

**60-minute boil: 1.25 ounces Tettnanger hops, divided into halves; 1.5 ounces Hallertau hops, divided into thirds**

**Ferment: 1 packet American ale yeast, such as Safale S-05; 1 cup maple syrup, for bottling**

- - - - - - - - - - - - - - -

## SUGGESTED FOOD PAIRINGS

· **Barbecued ribs**
· **Smoked fish**
· **Smoked meat**

**BERRY BEERS GET A BAD RAP AMONG BEER NERDS,** and it's somewhat understandable. Commercial versions can have a syrupy quality reminiscent of cough medicine. Don't be discouraged: Real berries can make a beer that's lovely and refreshing. Blackberries make perfect sense because they're tart and not overly sweet to begin with. Here, we give them a quick mash and melt them into an easy-drinking Irish Red Ale base. The fruit flavor hovers in the background, mingling with the hops' citrusy aroma for a distinctive late-summer beer. You can use cherries or blueberries in place of the blackberries.

# BLACKBERRY RED ALE
## 6.0% ABV

### BLACKBERRY MIXTURE

1 cup fresh blackberries
¼ cup sugar

### 60-MINUTE MASH AT 152°F

2 quarts water, plus 1 gallon for sparging
1.45 pounds Maris Otter malt
0.35 pound Caramel 60 malt
0.13 pound Aromatic malt
*all grains should be milled (see note, page 17)

### 60-MINUTE BOIL

0.25 ounce East Kent Golding hops, divided into halves
0.13 ounce Cascade hops

### FERMENT

½ packet English ale yeast, such as Nottingham (see note, page 22)
3 tablespoons honey, for bottling

**TO MAKE THE BLACKBERRY MIXTURE:** In a heavy-bottomed saucepan on low heat, mash the blackberries and the sugar together with a fork. Stir until the blackberries dissolve into a syrup, about 5 minutes. Let cool.

**MASH:** In a medium stockpot, heat the 2 quarts water over high heat to 160°F. Add all the malts and stir gently. The temperature should reduce to 150°F within 1 minute. Turn off the heat. Steep the grains for 60 minutes between 144°F and 152°F. Every 10 minutes, stir and take the temperature. If the grains get too cold, turn on the heat to high while stirring until the temperature rises to that range, then turn off the heat. With 10 minutes left, in a second medium stockpot heat the 1 gallon water to 170°F. After the grains have steeped for 60 minutes, raise the heat of the grains-and-water mixture to high and stir until the temperature reaches 170°F. Turn off the heat.

**SPARGE:** Place a fine-mesh strainer over a pot, and pour the grains into the strainer, reserving the liquid. Pour the 1 gallon of 170°F water over the grains. Recirculate the collected liquid through the grains once.

**BOIL:** Return the pot with the liquid to the stove on high heat and bring to a boil. When it starts to foam, reduce the heat to a slow rolling boil and add half of the East Kent Golding hops. Add the remaining East Kent Golding hops after 30 minutes and the Cascade hops after 55 minutes. Prepare an ice bath by stopping the sink and filling it with 5 inches of water and ice. At the 60-minute mark, turn off the heat, add the blackberry mixture, and stir to dissolve. Place the pot in the ice bath in the sink and cool to 70°F, about 30 minutes.

**FERMENT:** Using a sanitized funnel and strainer, pour the liquid into a sanitized fermenter. Add any water needed to fill the jug to the 1-gallon mark. Add the yeast, sanitize your hands, cover the mouth of the jug with one hand, and shake to distribute evenly. Attach a sanitized stopper and tubing to the fermenter and insert the other end of the tubing into a small bowl of sanitizing solution. The solution will begin to bubble as the yeast activates, pushing gas through the tube. Wait 2 to 3 days until the bubbling has slowed, then replace the tubing system with an airlock (see page 28). Wait 11 more days, then bottle, using the honey (see page 30 for bottling instructions).

## FOR 5 GALLONS

**Blackberry mixture:** 5 cups blackberries; 1¼ cups sugar

**60-minute mash at 152°F:** 2½ gallons water, plus 5 gallons for sparging; 7.25 pounds Maris Otter malt, 1.75 pounds Caramel 60 malt, 0.65 pound Aromatic malt

**60-minute boil:** 1.25 ounces East Kent Golding hops, divided into halves; 0.65 ounce Cascade hops

**Ferment:** 1 packet English ale yeast, such as Nottingham; 1 cup honey, for bottling

- - - - - - - - - - - - - -

## SUGGESTED FOOD PAIRINGS

- **Grilled chicken**
- **Green salad with grapefruit**
- **Popovers**

**THIS SUMMERTIME I.P.A.** is made exclusively with Simcoe hops, a relatively new variety developed in the Pacific Northwest. A light, crisp base provides the perfect showcase for the hops' distinctive aroma, which carries notes of tropical fruit and pine. It's a great beer for outdoor adventures.

# SIMCOE I.P.A. 7.6% ABV

### 60-MINUTE MASH AT 152°F

3 quarts water, plus 1 gallon for sparging

2.3 pounds Belgian Pilsner malt

0.5 pound Caravienne malt

0.1 pound Biscuit malt

0.1 pound Aromatic malt

*all grains should be milled (see note, page 17)

### 60-MINUTE BOIL

0.6 ounce Simcoe hops, divided into sixths

### FERMENT

½ packet English ale yeast, such as Safale S-04 (see note, page 22)

3 tablespoons honey, for bottling

**MASH:** In a medium stockpot, heat the 3 quarts water over high heat to 160°F. Add all the malts and stir gently. The temperature should reduce to 150°F within 1 minute. Turn off the heat. Steep the grains for 60 minutes between 144°F and 152°F. Every 10 minutes, stir and take the temperature. If the grains get too cold, turn on the heat to high while stirring until the temperature rises to that range, then turn off the heat. With 10 minutes left, in a second medium stockpot heat the 1 gallon water to 170°F. After the grains have steeped for 60 minutes, raise the heat of the grains-and-water mixture to high and stir until the temperature reaches 170°F. Turn off the heat.

**SPARGE:** Place a fine-mesh strainer over a pot, and pour the grains into the strainer, reserving the liquid. Pour the 1 gallon of 170°F water over the grains. Recirculate the collected liquid through the grains once.

**BOIL:** Return the pot with the liquid to the stove on high heat and bring to a boil. When it starts to foam, reduce the heat to a slow rolling boil and add one sixth of the Simcoe hops. Add another sixth of the hops after 15 minutes, 30 minutes, 45 minutes, and 55 minutes. Prepare an ice bath by stopping the sink and filling it with 5 inches of water and ice. At the 60-minute mark, turn off the heat and add the remaining hops. Place the pot in the ice bath in the sink and cool to 70°F, about 30 minutes.

**FERMENT:** Using a sanitized funnel and strainer, pour the liquid into a sanitized fermenter. Add any water needed to fill the jug to the 1-gallon mark. Add the yeast, sanitize your hands, cover the mouth of the jug with one hand, and shake to distribute evenly. Attach a sanitized stopper and tubing to the fermenter and insert the other end of the tubing into a small bowl of sanitizing solution. The solution will begin to bubble as the yeast activates, pushing gas through the tube. Wait 2 to 3 days until the bubbling has slowed, then replace the tubing system with an airlock (see page 28). Wait 11 more days, then bottle, using the honey (see page 30 for bottling instructions).

**Variation:** Since this recipe only calls for one type of hop, it's a great base to use if you want to see how different hops taste. Centennial, Chinook, and Cascade make terrific single-hop beers.

## FOR 5 GALLONS

**60-minute mash at 152°F: 3¾ gallons water, plus 5 gallons for sparging; 11.5 pounds Belgian Pilsner malt, 2.5 pounds Caravienne malt, 0.5 pound Biscuit malt, 0.5 pound Aromatic malt**

**60-minute boil: 3 ounces Simcoe hops, divided into sixths**

**Ferment: 1 packet English ale yeast, such as Safale S-04; 1 cup honey, for bottling**

## SUGGESTED FOOD PAIRINGS

- **Potato salad**
- **Grilled shrimp**
- **Corn chowder**

SINCE JALAPEÑOS ARE OFTEN USED IN COOKING SIMPLY FOR THEIR SPICINESS, we tend to forget that they also have a great fresh flavor. In this recipe, we push the heat to the background to let the bright green snappiness of pepper shine through. There's a gentle kick for sure in this mild version, but if you're looking for more heat, brew the spicy one (page 78).

# JALAPEÑO SAISON MILD 6.0% ABV

## 60-MINUTE MASH AT 152°F

2½ quarts water, plus 1 gallon for sparging

2.2 pounds Belgian Pilsner malt

0.2 pound Caramel 20 malt

*all grains should be milled (see note, page 17)

## 60-MINUTE BOIL

0.1 ounce Pacific Jade hops

0.16 ounce Spaltz hops, divided into halves

1 jalapeño pepper, seeded and chopped

## FERMENT

½ packet Belgian ale yeast, such as Wyeast Belgian Saison or Safbrew T-58 (see note, page 22)

3 tablespoons agave nectar, for bottling

**MASH:** In a medium stockpot, heat the 2½ quarts water over high heat to 160°F. Add all the malts and stir gently. The temperature should reduce to 150°F within 1 minute. Turn off the heat. Steep the grains for 60 minutes between 144°F and 152°F. Every 10 minutes, stir and take the temperature. If the grains get too cold, turn on the heat to high while stirring until the temperature rises to that range, then turn off the heat. With 10 minutes left, in a second medium stockpot heat the 1 gallon water to 170°F. After the grains have steeped for 60 minutes, raise the heat of the grains-and-water mixture to high and stir until the temperature reaches 170°F. Turn off the heat.

**SPARGE:** Place a fine-mesh strainer over a pot, and pour the grains into the strainer, reserving the liquid. Pour the 1 gallon of 170°F water over the grains. Recirculate the collected liquid through the grains once.

**BOIL:** Return the pot with the liquid to the stove on high heat and bring to a boil. When it starts to foam, reduce the heat to a slow rolling boil and add the Pacific Jade hops. Add half of the Spaltz hops after 30 minutes, the chopped jalapeño after 50 minutes, and the remaining Spaltz hops after 55 minutes. Prepare an ice bath by stopping the sink and filling it with 5 inches of water and ice. At the 60-minute mark, turn off the heat. Place the pot in the ice bath in the sink and cool to 70°F, about 30 minutes.

**FERMENT:** Using a sanitized funnel and strainer, pour the liquid into a sanitized fermenter. Add any water needed to fill the jug to the 1-gallon mark. Add the yeast, sanitize your hands, cover the mouth of the jug with one hand, and shake to distribute evenly. Attach a sanitized stopper and tubing to the fermenter and insert the other end of the tubing into a small bowl of sanitizing solution. The solution will begin to bubble as the yeast activates, pushing gas through the tube. Wait 2 to 3 days until the bubbling has slowed, then replace the tubing system with an airlock (see page 28). Wait 11 more days, then bottle, using the agave nectar (see page 30 for bottling instructions).

## FOR 5 GALLONS

**60-minute mash at 152°F: 3 gallons water, plus 5 gallons for sparging; 11 pounds Belgian Pilsner malt, 1 pound Caramel 20 malt**

**60-minute boil: 0.5 ounce Pacific Jade hops; 0.8 ounce Spaltz hops, divided into halves; 5 jalapeños, seeded and chopped**

**Ferment: 1 packet Belgian ale yeast, such as Wyeast Belgian Saison or Safbrew T-58; 1 cup agave nectar, for bottling**

## SUGGESTED FOOD PAIRINGS

- **Watermelon salad**
- **Mango**
- **Gazpacho**

**ERICA LIKES THINGS SUPER-SPICY—LIKE TEARS-RUNNING-DOWN-HER-FACE SPICY—**so we designed a beer that could provide a challenge. Making spicy beers isn't just about adding more peppers when you want more heat: We had to come up with an entirely different architecture than what's used for the Jalapeño Saison Mild (page 76). There's still just one pepper per gallon, but here, the extra sugar (and therefore extra alcohol) helps to amplify the spiciness. Consider yourself warned.

# JALAPEÑO SAISON SPICY 6.2% ABV

### 60-MINUTE MASH AT 152°F

1¾ quarts water, plus 1 gallon for sparging

1.6 pounds Belgian Pilsner malt

0.1 pound Aromatic malt

0.02 pound Munich malt

*all grains should be milled (see note, page 17)

### 60-MINUTE BOIL

0.08 ounce Pacific Jade hops, divided into halves

0.12 ounce Sorachi hops, divided into thirds

1 jalapeño pepper, chopped, with seeds

0.2 pound clear Belgian Candi Sugar (see note, page 22)

⅓ cup agave nectar

### FERMENT

½ packet Belgian ale yeast, such as Wyeast Belgian Saison or Safbrew T-58 (see note, page 22)

3 tablespoons agave nectar, for bottling

**MASH:** In a medium stockpot, heat the 1¾ quarts water over high heat to 160°F. Add all the malts and stir gently. The temperature should reduce to 150°F within 1 minute. Turn off the heat. Steep the grains for 60 minutes between 144°F and 152°F. Every 10 minutes, stir and take the temperature. If the grains get too cold, turn on the heat to high while stirring until the temperature rises to that range, then turn off the heat. With 10 minutes left, in a second medium stockpot heat the 1 gallon water to 170°F. After the grains have steeped for 60 minutes, raise the heat of the grains-and-water mixture to high and stir until the temperature reaches 170°F. Turn off the heat.

**SPARGE:** Place a fine-mesh strainer over a pot, and pour the grains into the strainer, reserving the liquid. Pour the 1 gallon of 170°F water over the grains. Recirculate the collected liquid through the grains once.

**BOIL:** Return the pot with the liquid to the stove on high heat and bring to a boil. When it starts to foam, reduce the heat to a slow rolling boil and add half of the Pacific Jade hops. Add the remaining Pacific Jade hops after 30 minutes, one third of the Sorachi hops after 45 minutes, the chopped jalapeño after 50 minutes, and another third of the Sorachi hops after 55 minutes. Prepare an ice bath by stopping the sink and filling it with 5 inches of water and ice. At the 60-minute mark, turn off the heat, add the remaining Sorachi hops, the Belgian Candi Sugar, and the agave nectar, and stir to dissolve the sugar. Place the pot in the ice bath in the sink and cool to 70°F, about 30 minutes.

**FERMENT:** Using a sanitized funnel and strainer, pour the liquid into a sanitized fermenter. Add any water needed to fill the jug to the 1-gallon mark. Add the yeast, sanitize your hands, cover the mouth of the jug with one hand, and shake to distribute evenly. Attach a sanitized stopper and tubing to the fermenter and insert the other end of the tubing into a small bowl of sanitizing solution. The solution will begin to bubble as the yeast activates, pushing gas through the tube. Wait 2 to 3 days until the bubbling has slowed, then replace the tubing system with an airlock (see page 28). Wait 11 more days, then bottle, using the agave nectar (see page 30 for bottling instructions).

## FOR 5 GALLONS

**60-minute mash at 152°F: 2¼ gallons water, plus 5 gallons for sparging; 8 pounds Belgian Pilsner malt, 0.5 pound Aromatic malt, 0.1 pound Munich malt**

**60-minute boil: 0.4 ounce Pacific Jade hops, divided into halves; 0.6 ounce Sorachi hops, divided into thirds; 5 jalapeños, chopped; 1 pound clear Belgian Candi Sugar; 1²/₃ cups agave nectar**

**Ferment: 1 packet Belgian ale yeast, such as Wyeast Belgian Saison or Safbrew T-58; 1 cup agave nectar, for bottling**

- - - - - - - - - - - - - - -

## SUGGESTED FOOD PAIRINGS

- **Nachos**
- **Ceviche**
- **Fish tacos**

**CHERRY ALES COME FROM A LONG TRADITION OF TOSSING EXTRA ORCHARD FRUIT INTO FERMENTING BEERS.** Here we brew with smoked cherrywood malt, which is smoother and sweeter than peat or beechwood smoked malts. Place the whole cherries directly into the fermenter. They'll melt slowly into the beer, creating an almost brandy-like flavor. This beer really comes into its own after about six months in bottles, if you can wait that long to drink it (see Aging Beers, page 137).

# SMOKED **CHERRY**
## 6.3% ABV

### 60-MINUTE MASH AT 152°F

2½ quarts water, plus 1 gallon for sparging

1.6 pounds Maris Otter malt

0.6 pound Cherrywood Smoked malt

0.1 pound Caramel 40 malt

0.1 pound Victory malt

*all grains should be milled (see note, page 17)

### 60-MINUTE BOIL

0.2 ounce Brambling Cross hops

0.15 ounce Whitbread Golding hops, divided into thirds

1 cup pitted fresh cherries

### FERMENT

½ packet American ale yeast, such Safale S-05 (see note, page 22)

3 tablespoons honey, for bottling

**MASH:** In a medium stockpot, heat the 2½ quarts water over high heat to 160°F. Add all the malts and stir gently. The temperature should reduce to 150°F within 1 minute. Turn off the heat. Steep the grains for 60 minutes between 144°F and 152°F. Every 10 minutes, stir and take the temperature. If the grains get too cold, turn on the heat to high while stirring until the temperature rises to that range, then turn off the heat. With 10 minutes left, in a second medium stockpot heat the 1 gallon water to 170°F. After the grains have steeped for 60 minutes, raise the heat of the grains-and-water mixture to high and stir until the temperature reaches 170°F. Turn off the heat.

**SPARGE:** Place a fine-mesh strainer over a pot, and pour the grains into the strainer, reserving the liquid. Pour the 1 gallon of 170°F water over the grains. Recirculate the collected liquid through the grains once.

**BOIL:** Return the pot with the liquid to the stove on high heat and bring to a boil. When it starts to foam, reduce the heat to a slow rolling boil and add the Brambling Cross hops. Add one third of the Whitbread Golding hops after 45 minutes and another third of the Whitbread Golding hops after 55 minutes. Prepare an ice bath by stopping the sink and filling it with 5 inches of water and ice. At the 60-minute mark, turn off the heat, add the remaining Whitbread Golding hops and the cherries, and stir to combine. Place the pot in the ice bath in the sink and cool to 70°F, about 30 minutes.

**FERMENT:** Using a sanitized funnel, pour the liquid and the cherries into a sanitized fermenter, trying to keep the hop sediment out. Add any water needed to fill the jug to the 1-gallon mark. Add the yeast, sanitize your hands, cover the mouth of the jug with one hand, and shake to distribute evenly. Attach a sanitized stopper and tubing to the fermenter and insert the other end of the tubing into a small bowl of sanitizing solution. The solution will begin to bubble as the yeast activates, pushing gas through the tube. Wait 2 to 3 days until the bubbling has slowed, then replace the tubing system with an airlock (see page 28). Wait 11 more days, then bottle, using the honey (see page 30 for bottling instructions).

## FOR 5 GALLONS

**60-minute mash at 152°F: 3 gallons water, plus 5 gallons for sparging; 8 pounds Maris Otter malt, 3 pounds Cherrywood Smoked malt, 0.5 pound Caramel 40 malt, 0.5 pound Victory malt**

**60-minute boil: 1 ounce Brambling Cross hops; 0.75 ounce Whitbread Golding hops, divided into thirds; 5 cups pitted fresh cherries**

**Ferment: 1 packet American ale yeast, such Safale S-05; 1 cup honey, for bottling**

- - - - - - - - - - - - -

## SUGGESTED FOOD PAIRINGS

- **Grilled meats**
- **Panna cotta**
- **Soft washed-rind cheeses**

**THINK OF THIS AS MORE OF A FIGURATIVE INTERPRETATION OF A S'MORE RATHER THAN A LITERAL ONE.** The roasty sweetness of caramel malts approximates the nutty flavor of graham crackers, while an English ale yeast adds a fluffy head that might remind you of a gooey marshmallow. Instead of using Chocolate malt for chocolate flavor, as we did in the Chocolate Maple Porter (page 138), we experimented with chocolate fines, the unprocessed shells and nibs of the cocoa bean. The shells have a touch of tannin and help to filter the beer for clarity, while the nibs add a chocolate flavor that's more fruity (think high-quality dark chocolate) than sweet. We like the chocolate fines from Taza Chocolate (see Sources, page 172).

# S'MORE BEER 7.0% ABV

### 60-MINUTE MASH AT 152°F

- 2¾ quarts water, plus 1 gallon for sparging
- 1.5 pounds Maris Otter malt
- 0.6 pound Smoked malt
- 0.2 pound Caramel 20 malt
- 0.2 pound Caramel 60 malt
- 0.2 pound Chocolate malt
- 1½ tablespoons chocolate fines (see headnote)
- *all grains should be milled (see note, page 17)

### 60-MINUTE BOIL

- 0.1 ounce Centennial hops
- 0.15 ounce Hallertau hops, divided into thirds
- 1½ tablespoons chocolate fines

### FERMENT

- ½ packet English ale yeast, such as Safale S-04 (see note, page 22)
- 3 tablespoons maple syrup, for bottling

**MASH:** In a medium stockpot, heat the 2¾ quarts water over high heat to 160°F. Add all the malts and the 1½ tablespoons chocolate fines and stir gently. The temperature should reduce to 150°F within 1 minute. Turn off the heat. Steep the grains for 60 minutes between 144°F and 152°F. Every 10 minutes, stir and take the temperature. If the grains get too cold, turn on the heat to high while stirring until the temperature rises to that range, then turn off the heat. With 10 minutes left, in a second medium stockpot heat the 1 gallon water to 170°F. After the grains have steeped for 60 minutes, raise the heat of the grains-and-water mixture to high and stir until the temperature reaches 170°F. Turn off the heat.

**SPARGE:** Place a fine-mesh strainer over a pot, and pour the grains into the strainer, reserving the liquid. Pour the 1 gallon of 170°F water over the grains. Recirculate the collected liquid through the grains once.

**BOIL:** Return the pot with the liquid to the stove on high heat and bring to a boil. When it starts to foam, reduce the heat to a slow rolling boil and add the Centennial hops. Add two thirds of the Hallertau hops after 30 minutes, the 1½ tablespoons chocolate fines after 45 minutes, and the remaining Hallertau hops after 55 minutes. Prepare an ice bath by stopping the sink and filling it with 5 inches of water and ice. At the 60-minute mark, turn off the heat. Place the pot in the ice bath in the sink and cool to 70°F, about 30 minutes.

**FERMENT:** Using a sanitized funnel and strainer, pour the liquid into a sanitized fermenter. Add any water needed to fill the jug to the 1-gallon mark. Add the yeast, sanitize your hands, cover the mouth of the jug with one hand, and shake to distribute evenly. Attach a sanitized stopper and tubing to the fermenter and insert the other end of the tubing into a small bowl of sanitizing solution. The solution will begin to bubble as the yeast activates, pushing gas through the tube. Wait 2 to 3 days until the bubbling has slowed, then replace the tubing system with an airlock (see page 28). Wait 11 more days, then bottle, using the maple syrup (see page 30 for bottling instructions).

## FOR 5 GALLONS

**60-minute mash at 152°F: 3½ gallons water, plus 5 gallons for sparging; 7.5 pounds Maris Otter malt, 3 pounds Smoked malt, 1 pound Caramel 20 malt, 1 pound Caramel 60 malt, 1 pound Chocolate malt; ½ cup chocolate fines**

**60-minute boil: 0.5 ounce Centennial hops; 0.75 ounce Hallertau hops, divided into thirds; ½ cup chocolate fines**

**Ferment: 1 packet English ale yeast, such as Safale S-04; 1 cup maple syrup, for bottling**

- - - - - - - - - - - - - - -

## SUGGESTED FOOD PAIRINGS

· **Vanilla ice cream**
· **Cheesecake with a graham cracker crust**
· **S'mores**

# AMONG THE MORE DELICIOUS-SOUNDING ADD-INS FOR BEER—

pepper, cloves, citrus—oysters rank nowhere near the top. But they're surprisingly terrific in stouts, a classic combination that we first encountered at Porter House, a brew pub in Dublin. Expecting the worst—or at least the weirdest—we were surprisingly won over by the roasted stout flavor with just a hint of brininess in the background. We borrowed the concept for this beer, but, with a nod to Erica's New England roots, we substituted a lobster shell for the oysters. Bay leaves and white peppercorns round out the mix to make a crisp, spicy, light saison with a mineral core that's perfect for any sort of seafood.

# LOBSTER SAISON
## 5.9% ABV

### PREP

1 lobster, boiled

### 60-MINUTE MASH AT 152°F

2¼ quarts water, plus 1 gallon for sparging

1.9 pounds Belgian Pilsner malt

0.2 pound Vienna malt

0.2 pound Aromatic malt

*all grains should be milled (see note, page 17)

### 60-MINUTE BOIL

0.3 ounce East Kent Golding hops, divided into thirds

2 bay leaves

5 white peppercorns

0.2 ounce Saaz hops

### FERMENT

½ packet Belgian ale yeast, such as Safale T-58 or Wyeast Belgian Saison (see note, page 22)

3 tablespoons honey, for bottling

**PREP:** Preheat the oven to 250°F. After cleaning out all the lobster meat, discard the head and legs, reserving the shell of the tail, body, and claws. Rinse the shells clean. Cook the shells in the oven on a baking sheet until they are dry, about 10 minutes.

**MASH:** In a medium stockpot, heat the 2¼ quarts water over high heat to 160°F. Add all the malts and stir gently. The temperature should reduce to 150°F within 1 minute. Turn off the heat. Steep the grains for 60 minutes between 144°F and 152°F. Every 10 minutes, stir and take the temperature. If the grains get too cold, turn on the heat to high while stirring until the temperature rises to that range, then turn off the heat. With 10 minutes left, in a second medium stockpot heat the 1 gallon water to 170°F. After the grains have steeped for 60 minutes, raise the heat of the grains-and-water mixture to high and stir until the temperature reaches 170°F. Turn off the heat.

**SPARGE:** Place a fine-mesh strainer over a pot, and pour the grains into the strainer, reserving the liquid. Pour the 1 gallon of 170°F water over the grains. Recirculate the collected liquid through the grains once.

**BOIL:** Return the pot with the liquid to the stove on high heat and bring to a boil. When it starts to foam, reduce the heat to a slow rolling boil and add one third of the East Kent Golding hops. After 30 minutes, add the remaining East Kent Golding hops, the lobster shells, bay leaves, and peppercorns, and after 58 minutes add the Saaz hops. Prepare an ice bath by stopping the sink and filling it with 5 inches of water and ice. At the 60-minute mark, turn off the heat. Place the pot in the ice bath in the sink and cool to 70°F, about 30 minutes.

**FERMENT:** Using a sanitized funnel and strainer, pour the liquid into a sanitized fermenter. Add any water needed to fill the jug to the 1-gallon mark. Add the yeast, sanitize your hands, cover the mouth of the jug with one hand, and shake to distribute evenly. Attach a sanitized stopper and tubing to the fermenter and insert the other end of the tubing into a small bowl of sanitizing solution. The solution will begin to bubble as the yeast activates, pushing gas through the tube. Wait 2 to 3 days until the bubbling has slowed, then replace the tubing system with an airlock (see page 28). Wait 11 more days, then bottle, using the honey (see page 30 for bottling instructions).

## FOR 5 GALLONS

**Prep: 3 lobsters, boiled**

**60-minute mash at 152°F: 3 gallons water, plus 5 gallons for sparging; 9.5 pounds Belgian Pilsner malt, 1 pound Vienna malt, 1 pound Aromatic malt**

**60-minute boil: 1.5 ounces East Kent Golding hops, divided into thirds; 5 bay leaves; 2 tablespoons white peppercorns; 1 ounce Saaz hops**

**Ferment: 1 packet Belgian ale yeast, such as Wyeast Belgian Saison or Safale T-58; 1 cup honey, for bottling**

- - - - - - - - - - - - - -

## SUGGESTED FOOD PAIRINGS

- **Lobster rolls**
- **Clambakes**
- **Buttered popcorn**

## WITH FLAKED OATS, BROWN SUGAR, AND ROASTED PEACHES,

this beer has all the elements of a classic cobbler. But instead of a sweet finish, the sugars ferment quite dry, leaving a tart lemony core with just a hint of peach on the aftertaste. It's especially lovely in the late summer—ripe, juicy, and aromatic—a good complement for all of the fresh produce we haul home from the farmer's markets. You can drink it right away, but it benefits from a few extra weeks in the bottle to let the flavors harmonize (see Aging Beers, page 137).

# PEACH COBBLER ALE 6.0% ABV

### PREP

2 ripe peaches, peeled and halved, pits removed

### 60-MINUTE MASH AT 152°F

2 quarts water, plus 1 gallon for sparging

0.8 pound English Pale malt

0.6 pound Biscuit malt

0.2 pound Caramel 15 malt

0.2 pound Caramel 20 malt

0.15 pound flaked oats

*all grains should be milled (see note, page 17)

### 60-MINUTE BOIL

0.1 ounce Columbus hops

0.2 ounce Saaz hops, divided into halves

½ cup packed light brown sugar

### FERMENT

½ packet English ale yeast, such as Nottingham (see note, page 22)

3 tablespoons honey, for bottling

**PREP:** Preheat the oven to 400°F. Place the peach halves directly on a baking sheet lined with aluminum foil and bake on the lower rack for 30 minutes, or until brown.

**MASH:** In a medium stockpot, heat the 2 quarts water over high heat to 160°F. Add all the malts and oats and stir gently. The temperature should reduce to 150°F within 1 minute. Turn off the heat. Steep the grains for 60 minutes between 144°F and 152°F. Every 10 minutes, stir and take the temperature. If the grains get too cold, turn on the heat to high while stirring until the temperature rises to that range, then turn off the heat. With 10 minutes left, in a second medium stockpot heat the 1 gallon water to 170°F. After the grains have steeped for 60 minutes, raise the heat of the grains-and-water mixture to high and stir until the temperature reaches 170°F. Turn off the heat.

**SPARGE:** Place a fine-mesh strainer over a pot, and pour the grains into the strainer, reserving the liquid. Pour the 1 gallon of 170°F water over the grains. Recirculate the collected liquid through the grains once.

**BOIL:** Return the pot with the liquid to the stove on high heat and bring to a boil. When it starts to foam, reduce the heat to a slow rolling boil and add the Columbus hops. Add half of the Saaz hops after 30 minutes and the remaining Saaz hops after 59 minutes. At the 60-minute mark, turn off the heat and add the peaches and brown sugar. Stir to dissolve the sugar and let the mixture steep for 20 minutes. Prepare an ice bath by stopping the sink and filling it with 5 inches of water and ice. Remove the peaches with a sanitized slotted spoon and place the pot in the ice bath in the sink and cool to 70°F, about 20 minutes.

**FERMENT:** Using a sanitized funnel and strainer, pour the liquid into a sanitized fermenter. Add any water needed to fill the jug to the 1-gallon mark. Add the yeast, sanitize your hands, cover the mouth of the jug with one hand, and shake to distribute evenly. Attach a sanitized stopper and tubing to the fermenter and insert the other end of the tubing into a small bowl of sanitizing solution. The solution will begin to bubble as the yeast activates, pushing gas through the tube. Wait 2 to 3 days until the bubbling has slowed, then replace the tubing system with an airlock (see page 28). Wait 11 more days, then bottle, using the honey (see page 30 for bottling instructions).

## FOR 5 GALLONS

**Prep: 10 peaches, peeled and halved, pits removed**

**60-minute mash at 152°F: 2½ gallons water, plus 5 gallons for sparging; 4 pounds English Pale malt, 3 pounds Biscuit malt, 1 pound Caramel 15 malt, 1 pound Caramel 20 malt, 0.75 pound flaked oats**

**60-minute boil: 0.5 ounce Columbus hops; 1 ounce Saaz hops, divided into halves; 2½ cups packed light brown sugar**

**Ferment: 1 packet English ale yeast, such as Nottingham; 1 cup honey, for bottling**

- - - - - - - - - - - - -

## SUGGESTED FOOD PAIRINGS

- **Green salads**
- **Prosciutto**
- **Ricotta**

## JUNIPER BERRIES AND CORIANDER IN TANDEM ARE THE CLASSIC AROMATICS FOR GIN.

They get used in beers, too, but more often on an individual basis (juniper in Scandinavian spiced ales and coriander in Belgian wits). Here, though, the pair adds joyous buoyancy to a strong Belgian ale, a light-bodied brew that packs a punch thanks to the addition of Belgian Candi Sugar. This almost tastes like a beer-gin cocktail, if you can imagine that—perfect for raising a special toast. Goes well with late nights and light foods of summer.

# BEL-GIN STRONG
## 7.25% ABV

### 60-MINUTE MASH AT 152°F

2½ quarts water, plus 1 gallon for sparging
2.0 pounds Belgian Pilsner malt
0.4 pound Caramel 10 malt
*all grains should be milled (see note, page 17)

### 60-MINUTE BOIL

0.12 ounce Northern Brewer hops
1 teaspoon juniper berries, crushed and divided into thirds
1 teaspoon dried coriander seeds, crushed and divided into thirds
0.3 ounce Saaz hops, divided into thirds
0.25 pound clear Belgian Candi Sugar (see note, page 22)

### FERMENT

½ packet Belgian ale yeast, such as Safale S-33 (see note, page 22)
3 tablespoons honey, for bottling

**MASH:** In a medium stockpot, heat the 2½ quarts water over high heat to 160°F. Add all the malts and stir gently. The temperature should reduce to 150°F within 1 minute. Turn off the heat. Steep the grains for 60 minutes between 144°F and 152°F. Every 10 minutes, stir and take the temperature. If the grains get too cold, turn on the heat to high while stirring until the temperature rises to that range, then turn off the heat. With 10 minutes left, in a second medium stockpot heat the 1 gallon water to 170°F. After the grains have steeped for 60 minutes, raise the heat of the grains-and-water mixture to high and stir until the temperature reaches 170°F. Turn off the heat.

**SPARGE:** Place a fine-mesh strainer over a pot, and pour the grains into the strainer, reserving the liquid. Pour the 1 gallon of 170°F water over the grains. Recirculate the collected liquid through the grains once.

**BOIL:** Return the pot with the liquid to the stove on high heat and bring to a boil. When it starts to foam, reduce the heat to a slow rolling boil and add the Northern Brewer hops, two thirds of the juniper berries, and two thirds of the coriander seeds. Add one third of the Saaz hops after 30 minutes and 45 minutes. Add the remaining Saaz hops, juniper berries, and coriander seeds after 55 minutes. Prepare an ice bath by stopping the sink and filling it with 5 inches of water and ice. At the 60-minute mark, turn off the heat, add the Belgian Candi Sugar, and stir to dissolve. Place the pot in the ice bath in the sink and cool to 70°F, about 30 minutes.

**FERMENT:** Using a sanitized funnel and strainer, pour the liquid into a sanitized fermenter. Add any water needed to fill the jug to the 1-gallon mark. Add the yeast, sanitize your hands, cover the mouth of the jug with one hand, and shake to distribute evenly. Attach a sanitized stopper and tubing to the fermenter and insert the other end of the tubing into a small bowl of sanitizing solution. The solution will begin to bubble as the yeast activates, pushing gas through the tube. Wait 2 to 3 days until the bubbling has slowed, then replace the tubing system with an airlock (see page 28). Wait 11 more days, then bottle, using the honey (see page 30 for bottling instructions).

## FOR 5 GALLONS

**60-minute mash at 152°F:
3¼ gallons water, plus
5 gallons for sparging;
10 pounds Belgian Pilsner
malt; 2 pounds Caramel
10 malt**

**60-minute boil: 0.6
ounce Northern Brewer
hops; 5 teaspoons juniper
berries, crushed and
divided into thirds;
5 teaspoons coriander
seeds, crushed and
divided into thirds;
1.5 ounces Saaz hops,
divided into thirds;
1.25 pounds clear Belgian
Candi Sugar**

**Ferment: 1 packet
Belgian ale yeast, such
as Safale S-33; 1 cup
honey, for bottling**

- - - - - - - - - - - - - -

## SUGGESTED FOOD PAIRINGS

- **Sushi**
- **Ceviche**
- **Pickled beets**

# A SUPER-REFRESHING BEER, PERFECT FOR THE HEIGHT OF SUMMER,

Kölsch is a German style of beer that uses ale yeast but is fermented at a cooler temperature typically used for lagers, resulting in a core of rich and fruity ale flavors wrapped up in a crisp and clean lager finish. You'll need somewhere cool (around 54°F) to properly finish the beer. A regular fridge is too cold, so we use a mini-fridge set to the right temperature.

# KÖLSCH

## 4.7% ABV

### 60-MINUTE MASH AT 152°F

2 quarts water, plus 1 gallon for sparging

1.5 pounds German Pilsner malt

0.25 pound Munich malt

0.2 pound Pale Wheat malt

*all grains should be milled (see note, page 17)

### 60-MINUTE BOIL

0.3 ounce Hallertau hops, divided into thirds

0.1 ounce Tettnanger hops

### FERMENT

½ packet German ale yeast, such as White Labs German Ale (see note, page 22)

3 tablespoons honey, for bottling

**Note:** If you don't have a mini-fridge, a cool basement or garage could work, too.

**MASH:** In a medium stockpot, heat the 2 quarts water over high heat to 160°F. Add all the malts and stir gently. The temperature should reduce to 150°F within 1 minute. Turn off the heat. Steep the grains for 60 minutes between 144°F and 152°F. Every 10 minutes, stir and take the temperature. If the grains get too cold, turn on the heat to high while stirring until the temperature rises to that range, then turn off the heat. With 10 minutes left, in a second medium stockpot heat the 1 gallon water to 170°F. After the grains have steeped for 60 minutes, raise the heat of the grains-and-water mixture to high and stir until the temperature reaches 170°F. Turn off the heat.

**SPARGE:** Place a fine-mesh strainer over a pot, and pour the grains into the strainer, reserving the liquid. Pour the 1 gallon of 170°F water over the grains. Recirculate the collected liquid through the grains once.

**BOIL:** Return the pot with the liquid to the stove on high heat and bring to a boil. When it starts to foam, reduce the heat to a slow rolling boil and add one third of the Hallertau hops. Add a third of the Halltertau hops after 15 minutes, another third after 40 minutes, and the Tettnanger hops after 58 minutes. Prepare an ice bath by stopping the sink and filling it with 5 inches of water and ice. At the 60-minute mark, turn off the heat. Place the pot in the ice bath in the sink and cool to 70°F, about 30 minutes.

**FERMENT:** Using a sanitized funnel and strainer, pour the liquid into a sanitized fermenter. Add any water needed to fill the jug to the 1-gallon mark. Add the yeast, sanitize your hands, cover the mouth of the jug with one hand, and shake to distribute evenly. Attach a sanitized stopper and tubing to the fermenter and insert the other end of the tubing into a small bowl of sanitizing solution. Place the fermenter in a storage area that is 54°F, such as a mini-fridge or cellar. The solution will begin to bubble as the yeast activates, pushing gas through the tube. Wait 2 to 3 days until the bubbling has slowed, then replace the tubing system with an airlock (see page 28). Wait 3 weeks, then siphon the beer into a second sanitized fermenter (or into a sanitized pot, then back into the cleaned fermenter). Store for 3 weeks at 35°F to 40°F (your regular refrigerator should work). After 6 weeks total, bottle, using the honey (see page 30 for bottling instructions). Store the bottles in your refrigerator, unless you decide to drink it all right away.

## FOR 5 GALLONS

**60-minute mash at 152°F: 2½ gallons water, plus 5 gallons for sparging; 7.5 pounds German Pilsner malt, 1.25 pounds Munich malt, 1 pound Pale Wheat malt**

**60-minute boil: 1.5 ounces Hallertau hops, divided into thirds; 0.5 ounce Tettnanger hops**

**Ferment: 1 packet German ale yeast, such as White Labs German Ale; 1 cup honey, for bottling**

- - - - - - - - - - - - - - -

## SUGGESTED FOOD PAIRINGS

- **Currywurst**
- **Onion rings**
- **Tamales**

# UNDER REGULAR CIRCUMSTANCES,

malting is something we'd happily leave to the professionals; they have better and more exacting equipment. But when it comes to developing gluten-free beers, malting our own grain opened a whole new world. The catalog of commercially malted grains is limited to mostly wheat, rye, and barley. We use buckwheat here, which can come pretty close to approximating the flavor of barley, but has no gluten. The gist of malting goes like this: Soak the seeds to sprout them, and then dry them out in an oven for about 60 minutes.

Red beets bring additional fermentable sugars, a tangy flavor, and a gorgeous pink color—perfect for the summer. Use young, tiny beets if you can. Their flavor is much sweeter and cleaner tasting than that of the larger, earthier types.

# GLUTEN-FREE BEET-BUCKWHEAT ALE 3.5% ABV

## PREP

1.4 pounds whole raw buckwheat (see note)

## 70-MINUTE MASH

1½ quarts water plus 1½ quarts, plus 1 gallon for sparging
0.2 pound rice hulls (see note, page 61)
1.4 pounds beets, peeled and grated

## 60-MINUTE BOIL

0.1 ounce East Kent Golding hops
0.2 ounce Amarillo hops, divided into halves
1 cup packed light brown sugar

## FERMENT

½ packet gluten-free ale yeast, such as Nottingham (see note, page 22)
3 tablespoons honey, for bottling

**Note:** Whole buckwheat is available at natural food stores. It is also referred to as "buckwheat berries."

**PREP:** Rinse the buckwheat, then cover in water and soak for 30 hours, changing the water and rinsing the grains every 8 hours. Strain, rinse once more, then leave the grains in a colander in the dark for 1 day, or until you see the grains begin to sprout. Let the grains sit until the sprouts have doubled in size, about 2 days. Preheat the oven to its lowest setting, or 200°F. Spread the grains over an unoiled rimmed baking sheet and bake for 60 minutes, or until the grains become dry. Rub the dried grains between your hands until the sprouted material falls away. Place the grains in a resealable plastic bag and crush with a rolling pin to "mill."

**MASH:** In a medium stockpot, heat the 1½ quarts water over high heat to 110°F. Add the buckwheat and stir gently. The temperature should drop to 95°F. Turn off the heat. Steep the grains for 15 minutes at 95°F, then turn the heat on high while stirring to raise the temperature to 113°F. Turn off the heat. Steep the grains for 15 minutes at 113°F, then add the rice hulls, the additional 1½ quarts water, and the beets and turn the heat on high while stirring to raise the temperature to 149°F, then turn off the heat. Steep the grains-beets mixture for 40 minutes at 149°F. Every 10 minutes, stir and take the temperature. If the grains-beets mixture gets too cold, turn on the heat to high while stirring until the temperature rises to 149°F, then turn off the heat. With 10 minutes left, in a second medium stockpot heat the 1 gallon of water to 150°F.

**RECIPE CONTINUES**

**SPARGE:** Place a fine-mesh strainer over a pot, and pour the grains and beets into the strainer, reserving the liquid. Pour the 1 gallon of 150°F water over the grains and beets. Recirculate the collected liquid through the grains and beets once.

**BOIL:** Return the pot with the liquid to the stove on high heat and bring to a boil. When it starts to foam, reduce the heat to a slow rolling boil and add the East Kent Golding hops. After 30 minutes, add half of the Amarillo hops. Prepare an ice bath by stopping the sink and filling it with 5 inches of water and ice. At the 60-minute mark, turn off the heat, add the remaining Amarillo hops and the sugar, and stir to dissolve the sugar. Place the pot in the ice bath in the sink and cool to 70°F, about 30 minutes.

**FERMENT:** Using a sanitized funnel and strainer, pour the liquid into a sanitized fermenter. Add any water needed to fill the jug to the 1-gallon mark. Add the gluten-free yeast, sanitize your hands, cover the mouth of the jug with one hand, and shake to distribute evenly. Attach a sanitized stopper and tubing to the fermenter and insert the other end of the tubing into a small bowl of sanitizing solution. The solution will begin to bubble as the yeast activates, pushing gas through the tube. Wait 2 to 3 days until the bubbling has slowed, then replace the tubing system with an airlock (see page 28). Wait 11 more days, then bottle, using the honey (see page 30 for bottling instructions).

## FOR 5 GALLONS

**Prep: 7 pounds whole raw buckwheat**

**70-minute mash: 2 gallons water, plus 5 gallons for sparging; 7 pounds peeled beets, grated; 0.5 pound rice hulls**

**60-minute boil: 0.5 ounce East Kent Golding hops; 1 ounce Amarillo hops, divided into halves; 5 cups packed light brown sugar**

**Ferment: 1 packet gluten-free ale yeast, such as Nottingham; 1 cup honey, for bottling**

– – – – – – – – – – – – – – –

## SUGGESTED FOOD PAIRINGS

· **Goat cheese**
· **Green salads**
· **Roasted nuts**

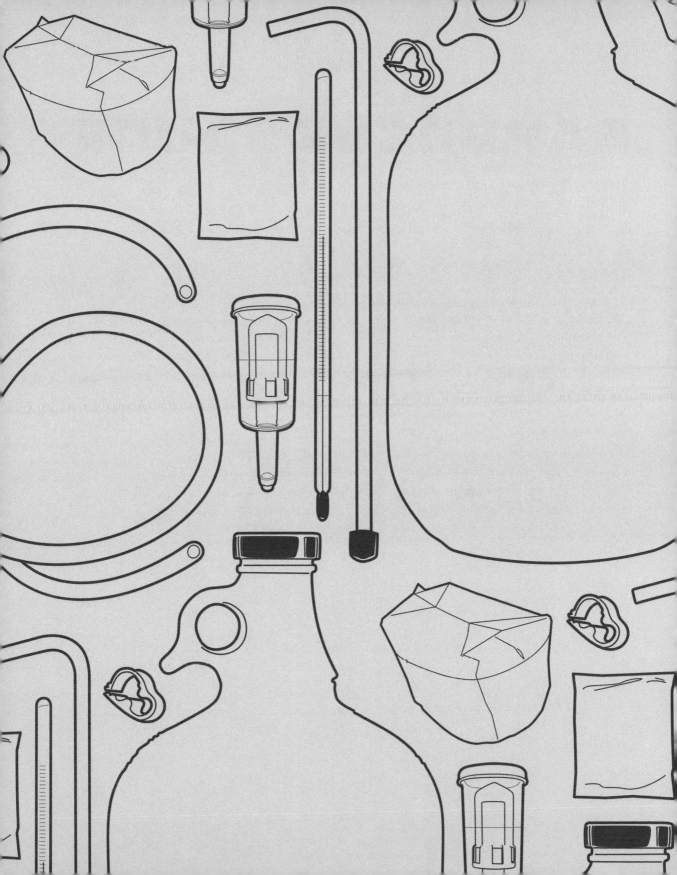

# BBQ BEER
# BARBECUE SAUCE

The smoky, roasted flavor of the beer makes a great contrast to the sweet ketchup in our favorite version of barbecue sauce. If you don't have the BBQ Beer on hand, a porter or a dubbel will work just as well.

**MAKES 3 cups**

1 cup dark beer, such as BBQ Beer (page 70), or Chocolate Maple Porter (page 138)

3 cups ketchup

2 tablespoons maple syrup

3 tablespoons fish sauce

3 tablespoons hot sauce, such as sriracha

Juice of ½ lime

1 bunch of scallions (green part only), cut on a bias into 1/2-inch strips

Salt and freshly ground black pepper

In a heavy-bottomed saucepan, cook the beer over medium heat until it has reduced to ¼ cup, about 15 minutes. Remove the beer from the heat and pour into a medium bowl. Stir in the ketchup, maple syrup, fish sauce, hot sauce, and lime juice until combined. Refrigerate for 60 minutes. Stir in the scallions and season with salt and pepper to taste.

# BEL-GIN STRONG BEER-BRINED PICKLES

We started making pickles by reusing the brine from pickles we had bought from McClure's at the Brooklyn Flea (and devoured halfway between weekend markets). After the brine got low, we started adding beer and experimenting with our own recipes. These pickles spiced with Bel-Gin Strong, juniper berries, and coriander make the perfect companion to burgers and grilled cheese sandwiches, but they're pretty great for snacking, too.

**MAKES 32 pickles**

8 Kirby cucumbers
1½ tablespoons kosher salt
5 tablespoons sugar
1 cup white wine vinegar

¼ cup Bel-Gin Strong (page 88), or any Belgian ale
1 tablespoon coriander seeds
½ tablespoon juniper berries

- - - - - - - - - - - - - - - - - - - - - - - - - - - - - - - - - - - - - - -

Cut the cucumbers in half lengthwise, then in half again to get four spears per cucumber. In a medium bowl, whisk together the salt, sugar, and vinegar until the sugar has dissolved. Add the beer, coriander seeds, and juniper berries to the mixture. Pack the cucumbers into a glass container with a tight-fitting lid (a clean reused pickle jar would be great) and pour the mixture over the cucumbers. Top off with cold water until the cucumbers are submerged. Refrigerate for 3 days before eating. These will last for 3 weeks in your fridge.

# FALL

**THERE'S A BRIEF MOMENT BETWEEN SUMMER AND FALL IN NEW YORK,** usually in September, when the last of the summer produce lines up alongside the muted oranges and yellows of the incoming fall roster. This is when it's best to be an eater in the city. There are still tomatoes for bruschetta, but there's also tender kale that hasn't grown tough yet in the cold. It's just chilly enough to start using your stove again, but still warm enough for rooftop barbecues.

It's also a tremendous time to brew beer. The markets are full of inspiration: pumpkins, apples, grapes, root vegetables, and cranberries. Spices and grains start to sound good again, too, adding subtle layers of warmth. Harvest time also signals the advent of traditional brewing celebrations, such as Oktoberfest.

We've included our favorite fall recipes in this section, the beers we think about brewing when that first tailgate rolls around, or for the last chilly backyard party. There are recipes here for the Thanksgiving table and even one to toast the anniversary of the end of Prohibition on December 5.

APPLE CRISP ALE

- - - - - - - - - - - - - - - - - - - - - - - - - - - - - - - - - - - - - - - - - - - - - - - - - - - - - - - - - - -

RYE P.A.

- - - - - - - - - - - - - - - - - - - - - - - - - - - - - - - - - - - - - - - - - - - - - - - - - - - - - - - - - - -

PROHIBITION ALE

- - - - - - - - - - - - - - - - - - - - - - - - - - - - - - - - - - - - - - - - - - - - - - - - - - - - - - - - - - -

IMPERIAL PEPPER STOUT

- - - - - - - - - - - - - - - - - - - - - - - - - - - - - - - - - - - - - - - - - - - - - - - - - - - - - - - - - - -

PEANUT BUTTER PORTER

- - - - - - - - - - - - - - - - - - - - - - - - - - - - - - - - - - - - - - - - - - - - - - - - - - - - - - - - - - -

CRANBERRY WHEAT

- - - - - - - - - - - - - - - - - - - - - - - - - - - - - - - - - - - - - - - - - - - - - - - - - - - - - - - - - - -

CARDAMOM ALE

- - - - - - - - - - - - - - - - - - - - - - - - - - - - - - - - - - - - - - - - - - - - - - - - - - - - - - - - - - -

OKTOBERFEST

- - - - - - - - - - - - - - - - - - - - - - - - - - - - - - - - - - - - - - - - - - - - - - - - - - - - - - - - - - -

A WELL-MADE TRIPEL

- - - - - - - - - - - - - - - - - - - - - - - - - - - - - - - - - - - - - - - - - - - - - - - - - - - - - - - - - - -

GRAPES & GRAINS ALE

- - - - - - - - - - - - - - - - - - - - - - - - - - - - - - - - - - - - - - - - - - - - - - - - - - - - - - - - - - -

MUSTARD BROWN ALE

- - - - - - - - - - - - - - - - - - - - - - - - - - - - - - - - - - - - - - - - - - - - - - - - - - - - - - - - - - -

PUMPKIN DUBBEL

- - - - - - - - - - - - - - - - - - - - - - - - - - - - - - - - - - - - - - - - - - - - - - - - - - - - - - - - - - -

GLUTEN-FREE PUMPKIN DUBBEL

- - - - - - - - - - - - - - - - - - - - - - - - - - - - - - - - - - - - - - - - - - - - - - - - - - - - - - - - - - -


BEER-BOILED PRETZEL BITES

- - - - - - - - - - - - - - - - - - - - - - - - - - - - - - - - - - - - - - - - - - - - - - - - - - - - - - - - - - -

BEER MUSTARD

- - - - - - - - - - - - - - - - - - - - - - - - - - - - - - - - - - - - - - - - - - - - - - - - - - - - - - - - - - -

MALTED APPLE ICE CREAM

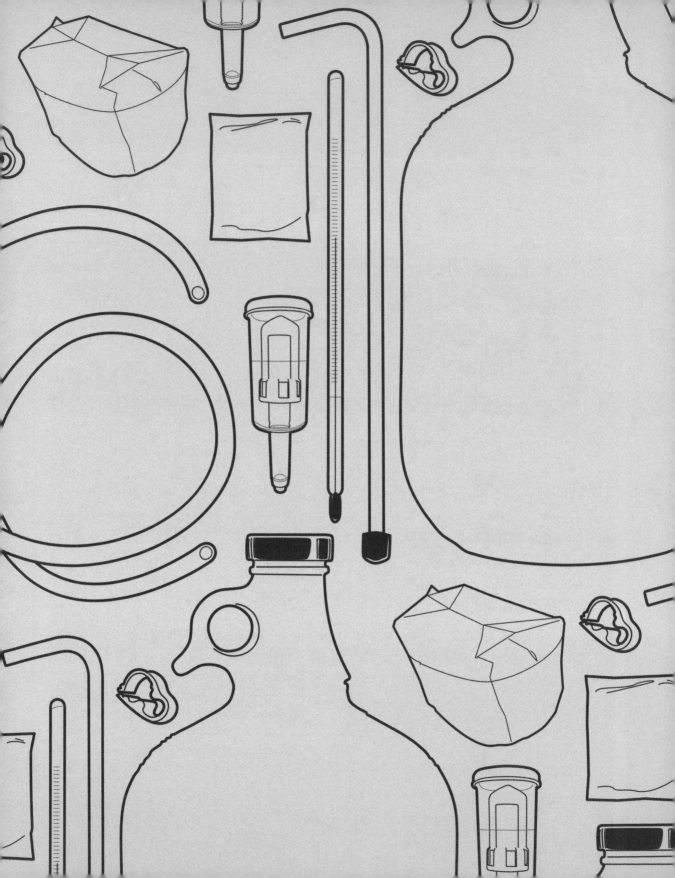

# FALL FEATURE
# KEEPING A KITCHEN GARDEN

We're always in denial about the first frost, but come September, it's time to move all the herbs indoors. We like to keep a mini–kitchen garden going through the winter. It gives us motivation for cooking and inspiration for brewing, too.

On our windowsill, we keep pots of rosemary, sage, tarragon, lavender, and thyme—all hardy, sturdy herbs that work well in brewing. Parsley, mint, and cilantro are good to have on hand for cooking, but aren't as good in beers.

1 Get pots that are bigger than you think you need—the herbs will be more vigorous with better root structure.

2 Keep them near the window so they can get natural sunlight, and don't forget to water them. Once every three days should be fine, unless your place is especially dry, and then try every other day.

3 If they start looking wan and shriveled, cover them with a clear plastic shopping bag for a few days. It will help concentrate warmth and moisture around the plants. Clip dead leaves and stalks back to help the plant continue to grow.

When you're ready to start experimenting with your own beers, herbs are a good place to start. You can add them as flavoring without having to do any of the calculations for fermentable sugars. Think of combinations you use in cooking: lemon and rosemary, or lavender and pepper, and give those a try.

**OUR PEACH COBBLER ALE** (page 86) worked so well in the summer that, naturally, we turned to apple crisp as the inspiration for fall. We wanted something light, slightly tart, and refreshing, more cider than sweet apple juice. We started with an American amber ale base of grains for a medium body with toasted flavor, but chose an English strain of yeast that brings a slight residual sweetness and a nice frothy head, making the apple aroma even more pronounced. We usually try to use one sweet apple and one tart to get a well-rounded apple flavor, but it changes every time depending on which varieties are at the market. The beer will take on the flavors of the apples you use, so choose apples that you like to eat.

# APPLE CRISP ALE
## 5.5% ABV

### 60-MINUTE MASH AT 152°F

2¼ quarts water, plus 1 gallon for sparging

2 pounds American 2-row malt

0.1 pound Caramel 60 malt

0.05 pound Chocolate malt

0.05 pound Aromatic malt

*all grains should be milled (see note, page 17)

### 60-MINUTE BOIL

0.3 ounce Fuggle hops

1 cinnamon stick

0.1 ounce Hallertau hops

2 apples, peeled and diced

### FERMENT

½ packet English ale yeast, such as Wyeast London III or Nottingham (see note, page 22)

3 tablespoons honey, for bottling

**Note:** Save the cooked apples after you take them out of the beer to make Malted Apple Ice Cream (page 133).

**MASH:** In a medium stockpot, heat the 2¼ quarts water over high heat to 160°F. Add all the malts and stir gently. The temperature should reduce to 150°F within 1 minute. Turn off the heat. Steep the grains for 60 minutes between 144°F and 152°F. Every 10 minutes, stir and take the temperature. If the grains get too cold, turn on the heat to high while stirring until the temperature rises to that range, then turn off the heat. With 10 minutes left, in a second medium stockpot heat the 1 gallon water to 170°F. After the grains have steeped for 60 minutes, raise the heat of the grains-and-water mixture to high and stir until the temperature reaches 170°F. Turn off the heat.

**SPARGE:** Place a fine-mesh strainer over a pot, and pour the grains into the strainer, reserving the liquid. Pour the 1 gallon of 170°F water over the grains. Recirculate the collected liquid through the grains once.

**BOIL:** Return the pot with the liquid to the stove on high heat and bring to a boil. When it starts to foam, reduce the heat to a slow rolling boil and add the Fuggle hops and cinnamon stick. Add the Hallertau hops after 59 minutes. At the 60-minute mark, turn off the heat and add the apples. Steep for 20 minutes. Prepare an ice bath by stopping the sink and filling it with 5 inches of water and ice. Remove the apples with a sanitized slotted spoon and place the pot in the ice bath in the sink and cool to 70°F, about 20 minutes.

**FERMENT:** Using a sanitized funnel and strainer, pour the liquid into a sanitized fermenter. Add any water needed to fill the jug to the 1-gallon mark. Add the yeast, sanitize your hands, cover the mouth of the jug with one hand, and shake to distribute evenly. Attach a sanitized stopper and tubing to the fermenter and insert the other end of the tubing into a small bowl of sanitizing solution. The solution will begin to bubble as the yeast activates, pushing gas through the tube. Wait 2 to 3 days until the bubbling has slowed, then replace the tubing system with an airlock (see page 28). Wait 11 more days, then bottle, using the honey (see page 30 for bottling instructions).

## FOR 5 GALLONS

**60-minute mash at 152°F: 3 gallons water, plus 5 gallons for sparging; 10 pounds American 2-row malt, 0.5 pound Caramel 60 malt; 0.25 pound Chocolate malt, 0.25 pound Aromatic malt**

**60-minute boil: 1.5 ounces Fuggle hops; 3 cinnamon sticks; 0.5 ounce Hallertau hops; 6 apples, peeled and diced**

**Ferment: 1 packet English ale yeast, such as Wyeast London III or Nottingham; 1 cup honey, for bottling**

## SUGGESTED FOOD PAIRINGS
- **Pork sausage**
- **Cheddar cheese**
- **Green salad**

# WHEN THE LEAVES START TO TURN FROM GREEN TO RED AND YOU FIND YOURSELF REACHING FOR SWEATERS AND FLANNEL,

the citrusy flavors of a traditional American I.P.A. can be a touch too bright and zingy. That's where our Rye P.A. comes in. It has the familiar bracing bitterness, but we've swapped in a more earthy set of hops. We also added a handful of rye into the grain mix. Rye can be tricky to brew with—it doesn't have the same structure as barley—but used in small doses like this, it adds a spicy character.

# RYE P.A.

## 6.5% ABV

### 60-MINUTE MASH AT 152°F

- 2½ quarts water, plus 1 gallon for sparging
- 1.8 pounds Maris Otter malt
- 0.4 pound Rye malt
- 0.16 pound Caramel 60 malt
- 0.1 pound Caramel 20 malt
- *all grains should be milled (see note, page 17)

### 60-MINUTE BOIL

- 0.3 ounce Northern Brewer hops, divided into halves
- 0.2 ounce Willamette hops, divided into quarters

### FERMENT

- ½ packet American ale yeast, such as Safale S-05 (see note, page 22)
- 3 tablespoons honey, for bottling

**MASH:** In a medium stockpot, heat the 2½ quarts water over high heat to 160°F. Add all the malts and stir gently. The temperature should reduce to 150°F within 1 minute. Turn off the heat. Steep the grains for 60 minutes between 144°F and 152°F. Every 10 minutes, stir and take the temperature. If the grains get too cold, turn on the heat to high while stirring until the temperature rises to that range, then turn off the heat. With 10 minutes left, in a second medium stockpot heat the 1 gallon water to 170°F. After the grains have steeped for 60 minutes, raise the heat of the grains-and-water mixture to high and stir until the temperature reaches 170°F. Turn off the heat.

**SPARGE:** Place a fine-mesh strainer over a pot, and pour the grains into the strainer, reserving the liquid. Pour the 1 gallon of 170°F water over the grains. Recirculate the collected liquid through the grains once.

**BOIL:** Return the pot with the liquid to the stove on high heat and bring to a boil. When it starts to foam, reduce the heat to a slow rolling boil and add half of the Northern Brewer hops. Add the remaining Northern Brewer hops after 15 minutes and one quarter of the Willamette hops after 30 minutes, 45 minutes, and 55 minutes. Prepare an ice bath by stopping the sink and filling it with 5 inches of water and ice. At the 60-minute mark, turn off the heat and add the remaining Willamette hops. Place the pot in the ice bath in the sink and cool to 70°F, about 30 minutes.

**FERMENT:** Using a sanitized funnel and strainer, pour the liquid into a sanitized fermenter. Add any water needed to fill the jug to the 1-gallon mark. Add the yeast, sanitize your hands, cover the mouth of the jug with one hand, and shake to distribute evenly. Attach a sanitized stopper and tubing to the fermenter and insert the other end of the tubing into a small bowl of sanitizing solution. The solution will begin to bubble as the yeast activates, pushing gas through the tube. Wait 2 to 3 days until the bubbling has slowed, then replace the tubing system with an airlock (see page 28). Wait 11 more days, then bottle, using the honey (see page 30 for bottling instructions).

## FOR 5 GALLONS

**60-minute mash at 152°F: 3 gallons water, plus 5 gallons for sparging; 9.0 pounds Maris Otter malt, 2 pounds Rye malt, 0.8 pound Caramel 60 malt, 0.5 pound Caramel 20 malt**

**60-minute boil: 1.5 ounces Northern Brewer hops, divided into halves; 1 ounce Willamette hops, divided into quarters**

**Ferment: 1 packet American ale yeast, such as Safale S-05; 1 cup honey, for bottling**

- - - - - - - - - - - -

## SUGGESTED FOOD PAIRINGS
- **Reuben sandwich**
- **Roasted cauliflower**
- **Smoked fish**

**ON ONE OF THE FIRST WEEKENDS WE SET UP SHOP AT THE BROOKLYN FLEA,** a spunky little old lady came up to our stand and told us about how she and her late husband brewed beer at home during Prohibition, using raisins to carbonate their beer in the bottle. The secret, she said, was getting the ratio right: with three raisins in each bottle, the beer would be flat, and with five, the bottles shattered from excess carbonation. This classic amber ale, medium-bodied and lightly malty, calls for the perfect ratio: four raisins. It is our tribute to the woman who taught us the raisin trick and to all the bootleggers who kept brewing alive. Brew this in the fall to be ready for December 5, the anniversary of the Twenty-first Amendment, which repealed Prohibition.

# PROHIBITION
# ALE
## 5.5% ABV

### 60-MINUTE MASH AT 152°F

2 quarts water, plus 1 gallon for sparging
1.6 pounds Maris Otter malt
0.4 pound Vienna malt
0.1 pound Special B malt
*all grains should be milled (see note, page 17)

### 60-MINUTE BOIL

0.25 ounce Brambling Cross hops, divided into halves
0.18 ounce Whitbread Golding hops, divided into thirds

### FERMENT

½ packet English ale yeast, such as Safale S-04 (see note, page 22)
40 raisins, for bottling

**MASH:** In a medium stockpot, heat the 2 quarts water over high heat to 160°F. Add all the malts and stir gently. The temperature should reduce to 150°F within 1 minute. Turn off the heat. Steep the grains for 60 minutes between 144°F and 152°F. Every 10 minutes, stir and take the temperature. If the grains get too cold, turn on the heat to high while stirring until the temperature rises to that range, then turn off the heat. With 10 minutes left, in a second medium stockpot heat the 1 gallon water to 170°F. After the grains have steeped for 60 minutes, raise the heat of the grains-and-water mixture to high and stir until the temperature reaches 170°F. Turn off the heat.

**SPARGE:** Place a fine-mesh strainer over a pot, and pour the grains into the strainer, reserving the liquid. Pour the 1 gallon of 170°F water over the grains. Recirculate the collected liquid through the grains once.

**BOIL:** Return the pot with the liquid to the stove on high heat and bring to a boil. When it starts to foam, reduce the heat to a slow rolling boil and add half of the Brambling Cross hops. Add the remaining Brambling Cross hops after 30 minutes and one third of the Whitbread Golding hops after 45 minutes and 55 minutes. Prepare an ice bath by stopping the sink and filling it with 5 inches of water and ice. At the 60-minute mark, turn off the heat and add the remaining Whitbread Golding hops. Place the pot in the ice bath in the sink and cool to 70°F, about 30 minutes.

**FERMENT:** Using a sanitized funnel and strainer, pour the liquid into a sanitized fermenter. Add any water needed to fill the jug to the 1-gallon mark. Add the yeast, sanitize your hands, cover the mouth of the jug with one hand, and shake to distribute evenly. Attach a sanitized stopper and tubing to the fermenter and insert the other end of the tubing into a small bowl of sanitizing solution. The solution will begin to bubble as the yeast activates, pushing gas through the tube. Wait 2 to 3 days until the bubbling has slowed, then replace the tubing system with an airlock (see page 28). Wait 11 more days, then bottle, using 4 raisins per bottle (see page 30 for bottling instructions). Raisins can take a bit longer than honey or maple syrup to carbonate your beer. Try one bottle of beer after 3 weeks. If carbonation is low wait 1 more week and try again.

## FOR 5 GALLONS

**60-minute mash at 152°F: 2½ gallons water, plus 5 gallons for sparging; 8 pounds Maris Otter malt, 2 pounds Vienna malt, 0.5 pound Special B malt**

**60-minute boil: 1.25 ounces Brambling Cross hops, divided into halves; 0.9 ounce Whitbread Golding hops, divided into thirds**

**Ferment: 1 packet English ale yeast, such as Safale S-04; 200 raisins, for bottling**

- - - - - - - - - - - - - -

## SUGGESTED FOOD PAIRINGS

- **Roasted poultry**
- **Spicy nuts**
- **Firm cheeses**

# WHEN YOU SEE "IMPERIAL" ON A LABEL, it means that the beer in question is stronger. Everything about this style means more: more grain, more boil time, more concentration of flavor, and more alcohol. These "more" beers can be tricky to navigate; it's easy to end up with sticky syrup. But when executed well and with a little restraint, the imperial style can be rewarding, and they are especially good come the colder weather. All the dark, rich malty flavors are concentrated in this beer's 90-minute boil, but a dash of black peppercorns brings the whole thing into focus, an exclamation point that anchors the beer to the dinner table.

# IMPERIAL PEPPER STOUT 10.5% ABV

## 60-MINUTE MASH AT 152°F

- 4 quarts water, plus 1 gallon for sparging
- 2.7 pounds American 2-row malt
- 0.4 pound Rye malt
- 0.2 pound Caramel 120 malt
- 0.1 pound Black Patent malt
- 0.1 pound Caramel 15 malt
- 0.3 pound flaked barley
- 0.2 pound roasted barley
- *all grains should be milled (see note, page 17)

## 90-MINUTE BOIL

- 0.2 ounce Challenger hops, divided into halves
- 5 tablespoons crushed black peppercorns
- 0.16 ounce Brambling Cross hops
- 0.3 ounce Pacific Jade hops, divided into thirds

## FERMENT

- ½ packet Belgian ale yeast, such as Safbrew T-58 (see note, page 22)
- 3 tablespoons maple syrup, for bottling

**MASH:** In a medium stockpot, heat the 4 quarts water over high heat to 160°F. Add the malts and barleys and stir gently. The temperature should reduce to 150°F within 1 minute. Turn off the heat. Steep the grains for 60 minutes between 144°F and 152°F. Every 10 minutes, stir and take the temperature. If the grains get too cold, turn on the heat to high while stirring until the temperature rises to that range, then turn off the heat. With 10 minutes left, in a second medium stockpot heat the 1 gallon water to 170°F. After the grains have steeped for 60 minutes, raise the heat of the grains-and-water mixture to high and stir until the temperature reaches 170°F. Turn off the heat.

**SPARGE:** Place a fine-mesh strainer over a pot, and pour the grains into the strainer, reserving the liquid. Pour the 1 gallon of 170°F water over the grains. Recirculate the collected liquid through the grains once.

**BOIL:** Return the pot with the liquid to the stove on high heat and bring to a boil. When it starts to foam, reduce the heat to a slow rolling boil and add half of the Challenger hops. Add the remaining Challenger hops after 30 minutes, 3 tablespoons of the black pepper after 45 minutes, the Brambling Cross hops after 60 minutes, the remaining black pepper after 70 minutes, one third of the Pacific Jade hops after 75 minutes, and another third after 85 minutes. Prepare an ice bath by stopping the sink and filling it with 5 inches of water and ice. At the 90-minute mark, turn off the heat and add the remaining Pacific Jade hops. Place the pot in the ice bath in the sink and cool to 70°F, at least 30 minutes.

**FERMENT:** Using a sanitized funnel and strainer, pour the liquid into a sanitized fermenter. Add any water needed to fill the jug to the 1-gallon mark. Add the yeast, sanitize your hands, cover the mouth of the jug with one hand, and shake to distribute evenly. Attach a sanitized stopper and tubing to the fermenter and insert the other end of the tubing into a small bowl of sanitizing solution. The solution will begin to bubble as the yeast activates, pushing gas through the tube. Wait 2 to 3 days until the bubbling has slowed, then replace the tubing system with an airlock (see page 28). Wait 11 more days, then bottle, using the maple syrup (see page 30 for bottling instructions).

## FOR 5 GALLONS

**60-minute mash at 152°F: 5 gallons water, plus 5 gallons for sparging; 13.5 pounds American 2-row malt, 2 pounds Rye malt, 1 pound Caramel 120 malt, 0.5 pound Black Patent malt, 0.5 pound Caramel 15 malt, 1.5 pounds flaked barley, 1 pound roasted barley**

**90-minute boil: 1 ounce Challenger hops, divided into halves; ½ cup crushed black peppercorns; 0.8 ounce Brambling Cross hops; 1.5 ounces Pacific Jade hops, divided into thirds**

**Ferment: 1 packet Belgian ale yeast, such as Safbrew T-58; 1 cup maple syrup, for bottling**

- - - - - - - - - - - - - - - -

## SUGGESTED FOOD PAIRINGS

- **Grilled red meat**
- **Aged cheddars**
- **Mustard greens**

# SOMEWHERE IN OUR COLLECTIVE CONSCIOUSNESS,

peanut butter registers as both a guilty pleasure (midnight snack) and a wholesome spread (PB&J). It's the stuff of Rockwellian Americana, a comforting land of cut-off crusts, swingsets, and bounding Labrador puppies. Here, peanut butter adds a cozy and reassuring warmth to a dark, creamy porter, perfect for colder fall nights. Natural peanut butter is essential in this recipe because of the separation of oil and nut paste. Let the oil settle out to the top and skim off the top inch or so. What you want to use is the dry, crumbly, chunky stuff at the bottom.

# PEANUT BUTTER PORTER

## 7.0% ABV

### 60-MINUTE MASH AT 152°F

3 quarts water, plus 1 gallon for sparging

2.4 pounds Pale Ale malt

0.2 pound Caramel 60 malt

0.1 pound Chocolate malt

0.2 pound roasted barley

*all grains should be milled (see note, page 17)

### 75-MINUTE BOIL

0.2 ounce Northern Brewer hops, divided into halves

⅓ cup natural peanut butter with the oil skimmed off

0.1 ounce Fuggle hops

### FERMENT

½ packet Belgian ale yeast, such as Safale S-33 (see note, page 22)

3 tablespoons maple syrup, for bottling

**MASH:** In a medium stockpot, heat the 3 quarts water over high heat to 160°F. Add all the malts and barley and stir gently. The temperature should reduce to 150°F within 1 minute. Turn off the heat. Steep the grains for 60 minutes between 144°F and 152°F. Every 10 minutes, stir and take the temperature. If the grains get too cold, turn on the heat to high while stirring until the temperature rises to that range, then turn off the heat. With 10 minutes left, in a second medium stockpot heat the 1 gallon water to 170°F. After the grains have steeped for 60 minutes, raise the heat of the grains-and-water mixture to high and stir until the temperature reaches 170°F. Turn off the heat.

**SPARGE:** Place a fine-mesh strainer over a pot, and pour the grains into the strainer, reserving the liquid. Pour the 1 gallon of 170°F water over the grains. Recirculate the collected liquid through the grains once.

**BOIL:** Return the pot with the liquid to the stove on high heat and bring to a boil. When it starts to foam, reduce the heat to a slow rolling boil and add half of the Northern Brewer hops. Add the peanut butter after 30 minutes, the remaining Northern Brewer hops after 45 minutes, and the Fuggle hops after 55 minutes. Prepare an ice bath by stopping the sink and filling it with 5 inches of water and ice. At the 75-minute mark, turn off the heat. Place the pot in the ice bath in the sink and cool to 70°F, about 30 minutes.

**FERMENT:** Using a sanitized funnel and strainer, pour the liquid into a sanitized fermenter. Add any water needed to fill the jug to the 1-gallon mark. Add the yeast, sanitize your hands, cover the mouth of the jug with one hand, and shake to distribute evenly. Attach a sanitized stopper and tubing to the fermenter and insert the other end of the tubing into a small bowl of sanitizing solution. The solution will begin to bubble as the yeast activates, pushing gas through the tube. Wait 2 to 3 days until the bubbling has slowed, then replace the tubing system with an airlock (see page 28). Wait 11 more days, then bottle, using the maple syrup (see page 30 for bottling instructions).

**Variation:** Try replacing peanut butter with other all-natural nut butters such as hazelnut or almond.

## FOR 5 GALLONS

**60-minute mash at 152°F: 3¾ gallons water, plus 5 gallons for sparging; 12 pounds Pale Ale malt, 1 pound Caramel 60 malt, 0.5 pound Chocolate malt, 1 pound roasted barley**

**75-minute boil: 1 ounce Northern Brewer hops, divided into halves; 1²/₃ cups peanut butter; 0.5 ounce Fuggle hops**

**Ferment: 1 packet Belgian ale yeast, such as Safale S-33; 1 cup maple syrup, for bottling**

- - - - - - - - - - - - - -

## SUGGESTED FOOD PAIRINGS

- **Apple desserts**
- **Vanilla ice cream**
- **Bananas Foster**

**ERICA ISN'T A HUGE FAN OF DESSERTS,** but she fell in love with a recipe for a cranberry tart from Babbo in New York City that was reprinted in the *New York Times*. She's made it for every Thanksgiving since she read it there. Here, we match the super-tart berries with a light wheat beer for a refreshing complement to our holiday spread. The bright red berries add a hint of red to the beer. We threw in some citrusy American hops and a fruity American yeast for the occasion.

# CRANBERRY WHEAT
## 5.0% ABV

### 60-MINUTE MASH AT 152°F

- 2 quarts water, plus 1 gallon for sparging
- 1 pound Pale Ale malt
- 0.7 pound Pale Wheat malt
- 0.2 pound Munich malt
- *all grains should be milled (see note, page 17)

### 60-MINUTE BOIL

- 0.08 ounce Chinook hops
- 0.2 ounce Amarillo hops, divided into halves
- 1 cup cranberries (fresh or frozen)

### FERMENT

- ½ packet American ale yeast, such as Safale S-05 (see note, page 22)
- 3 tablespoons honey, for bottling

**MASH:** In a medium stockpot, heat the 2 quarts water over high heat to 160°F. Add all the malts and stir gently. The temperature should reduce to 150°F within 1 minute. Turn off the heat. Steep the grains for 60 minutes between 144°F and 152°F. Every 10 minutes, stir and take the temperature. If the grains get too cold, turn on the heat to high while stirring until the temperature rises to that range, then turn off the heat. With 10 minutes left, in a second medium stockpot heat the 1 gallon water to 170°F. After the grains have steeped for 60 minutes, raise the heat of the grains-and-water mixture to high and stir until the temperature reaches 170°F. Turn off the heat.

**SPARGE:** Place a fine-mesh strainer over a pot, and pour the grains into the strainer, reserving the liquid. Pour the 1 gallon of 170°F water over the grains. Recirculate the collected liquid through the grains once.

**BOIL:** Return the pot with the liquid to the stove on high heat and bring to a boil. When it starts to foam, reduce the heat to a slow rolling boil and add the Chinook hops. Add half of the Amarillo hops after 30 minutes. Prepare an ice bath by stopping the sink and filling it with 5 inches of water and ice. At the 60-minute mark, turn off the heat and add the remaining Amarillo hops and the cranberries. Place the pot in the ice bath in the sink and cool to 70°F, about 30 minutes.

**FERMENT:** Using a sanitized funnel and strainer, pour the liquid into a sanitized fermenter. Add any water needed to fill the jug to the 1-gallon mark. Add the yeast, sanitize your hands, cover the mouth of the jug with one hand, and shake to distribute evenly. Attach a sanitized stopper and tubing to the fermenter and insert the other end of the tubing into a small bowl of sanitizing solution. The solution will begin to bubble as the yeast activates, pushing gas through the tube. Wait 2 to 3 days until the bubbling has slowed, then replace the tubing system with an airlock (see page 28). Wait 11 more days, then bottle, using the honey (see page 30 for bottling instructions).

## FOR 5 GALLONS

**60-minute mash at 152°F:**
**2½ gallons water, plus**
**5 gallons for sparging;**
**5 pounds Pale Ale malt,**
**3.5 pounds Pale Wheat**
**malt, 1 pound Munich**
**malt**

**60-minute boil:**
**0.4 ounce Chinook hops;**
**1 ounce Amarillo hops,**
**divided into halves;**
**5 cups cranberries**

**Ferment: 1 packet**
**American ale yeast, such**
**as Safale S-05; 1 cup**
**honey, for bottling**

- - - - - - - - - - - - - - -

## SUGGESTED FOOD PAIRINGS

- **Roasted turkey**
- **Stuffing**
- **Cranberry tart**

# WHEN WE'RE IN NEED OF INSPIRATION FOR NEW BEERS,

we rummage through the spice section of the Dual Specialty Store, an Indian spice store on First Avenue in Manhattan. Cardamom, a spice often used in Indian cooking, baking, and tea blends, has gorgeous, warm aromatics that fit in nicely with cool fall temperatures. Against a malty amber ale base, the green pods add notes of rich citrus, blood orange, and Meyer lemons, plus the sappy essence of fresh-cut pine and cedar. The Special B malt adds a hint of raisiny sweetness to the body.

# CARDAMOM ALE 5.1% ABV

### 60-MINUTE MASH AT 152°F

2 quarts water, plus 1 gallon for sparging

1.25 pounds Maris Otter malt

0.5 pound Munich malt

0.1 pound Special B malt

0.1 pound Vienna malt

*all grains should be milled (see note, page 17)

### 60-MINUTE BOIL

0.1 ounce Challenger hops

3 green cardamom seeds

0.4 ounce Willamette hops, divided into halves

### FERMENT

½ packet English ale yeast, such as Safale S-04 (see note, page 22)

3 tablespoons honey, for bottling

**MASH:** In a medium stockpot, heat the 2 quarts water over high heat to 160°F. Add all the malts and stir gently. The temperature should reduce to 150°F within 1 minute. Turn off the heat. Steep the grains for 60 minutes between 144°F and 152°F. Every 10 minutes, stir and take the temperature. If the grains get too cold, turn on the heat to high while stirring until the temperature rises to that range, then turn off the heat. With 10 minutes left, in a second medium stockpot, heat the 1 gallon water to 170°F. After the grains have steeped for 60 minutes, raise the heat of the grains-and-water mixture to high and stir until the temperature reaches 170°F. Turn off the heat.

**SPARGE:** Place a fine-mesh strainer over a pot, and pour the grains into the strainer, reserving the liquid. Pour the 1 gallon of 170°F water over the grains. Recirculate the collected liquid through the grains once.

**BOIL:** Return the pot with the liquid to the stove on high heat and bring to a boil. When it starts to foam, reduce the heat to a slow rolling boil and add the Challenger hops. Add the cardamom seeds and half of the Willamette hops after 30 minutes, and the remaining Willamette hops after 55 minutes. Prepare an ice bath by stopping the sink and filling it with 5 inches of water and ice. At the 60-minute mark, turn off the heat. Place the pot in the ice bath in the sink and cool to 70°F, about 30 minutes.

**FERMENT:** Using a sanitized funnel and strainer, pour the liquid into a sanitized fermenter. Add any water needed to fill the jug to the 1-gallon mark. Add the yeast, sanitize your hands, cover the mouth of the jug with one hand, and shake to distribute evenly. Attach a sanitized stopper and tubing to the fermenter and insert the other end of the tubing into a small bowl of sanitizing solution. The solution will begin to bubble as the yeast activates, pushing gas through the tube. Wait 2 to 3 days until the bubbling has slowed, then replace the tubing system with an airlock (see page 28). Wait 11 more days, then bottle, using the honey (see page 30 for bottling instructions).

**Variation:** Try swapping green with black cardamom seeds to give this beer a complex smokiness.

## FOR 5 GALLONS

**60-minute mash at 152°F: 2½ gallons water, plus 5 gallons for sparging; 6.25 pounds Maris Otter malt, 2.5 pounds Munich malt, 0.5 pound Special B malt, 0.5 pound Vienna malt**

**60-minute boil: 0.5 ounce Challenger hops; 15 cardamom seeds; 2 ounces Willamette hops, divided into halves**

**Ferment: 1 packet English ale yeast, such as Safale S-04; 1 cup honey, for bottling**

- - - - - - - - - - - - - -

## SUGGESTED FOOD PAIRINGS

· **Coconut curries**
· **Roasted lamb**
· **Eggplant**

## WE DON'T BREW A LOT OF LAGERS, but we make an exception for Oktoberfest.

The two-week-long festival in Germany, which is held in late September, originally started in the early nineteenth century as a wedding celebration for the royal family, but it has morphed into the largest and most famous beer festival in the world. It's a fun thing to celebrate, even if you're not in Munich. The Oktoberfest style, a malty full-bodied dark lager called Märzen, is a catchall category that leaves a lot of room to play around.

You'll need a cool place to ferment and store the beer; a regular-size refrigerator will be too cold, but a mini-fridge with an adjustable thermostat, or a cool cellar, will do the job. Transferring your beer to a second fermenter results in a clearer, less yeasty beer.

# OKTOBER-FEST 5.6% ABV

### 60-MINUTE MASH AT 152°F

- 2 quarts water, plus 1 gallon for sparging
- 1.2 pounds German Pilsner malt
- 0.6 pound Munich malt
- 0.3 pound Caravienne malt
- *all grains should be milled (see note, page 17)

### 60-MINUTE BOIL

- 0.1 ounce Perle hops
- 0.2 ounce Tettnanger hops, divided into halves

### FERMENT

- ½ packet German lager yeast, such as Wyeast Oktoberfest (see note, page 22)
- 3 tablespoons honey, for bottling

**MASH:** In a medium stockpot, heat the 2 quarts water over high heat to 160°F. Add all the malts and stir gently. The temperature should reduce to 150°F within 1 minute. Turn off the heat. Steep the grains for 60 minutes between 144°F and 152°F. Every 10 minutes, stir and take the temperature. If the grains get too cold, turn on the heat to high while stirring until the temperature rises to that range, then turn off the heat. With 10 minutes left, in a second medium stockpot, heat the 1 gallon water to 170°F. After the grains have steeped for 60 minutes, raise the heat of the grains-and-water mixture to high and stir until the temperature reaches 170°F. Turn off the heat.

**SPARGE:** Place a fine-mesh strainer over a pot, and pour the grains into the strainer, reserving the liquid. Pour the 1 gallon of 170°F water over the grains. Recirculate the collected liquid through the grains once.

**BOIL:** Return the pot with the liquid to the stove on high heat and bring to a boil. When it starts to foam, reduce the heat to a slow rolling boil and add the Perle hops. Add half of the Tettnanger hops after 30 minutes, and the remaining Tettnanger hops after 45 minutes. Prepare an ice bath by stopping the sink and filling it with 5 inches of water and ice. At the 60-minute mark, turn off the heat. Place the pot in the ice bath in the sink and cool to 70°F, about 30 minutes.

**FERMENT:** Using a sanitized funnel and strainer, pour the liquid into a sanitized fermenter. Add any water needed to fill the jug to the 1-gallon mark. Add the yeast, sanitize your hands, cover the mouth of the jug with one hand, and shake to distribute evenly. Attach a sanitized stopper and tubing to the fermenter and insert the other end of the tubing into a small bowl of sanitizing solution. Put the fermenter in cool storage at 54°F. The solution will begin to bubble as the yeast activates, pushing gas through the tube. Wait 2 to 3 days until the bubbling has slowed, then replace the tubing system with an airlock (see page 28). Wait 3 weeks, then siphon the beer into a second sanitized fermenter (or into a sanitized pot, then back into the cleaned fermenter). Store for 3 weeks at 35°F to 40°F (your regular refrigerator should work). After 6 weeks total, bottle, using the honey (see page 30 for bottling instructions). Store the bottles in a mini-fridge or your basement, unless, of course, you decide to drink it all right away.

## FOR 5 GALLONS

**60-minute mash at 152°F: 2½ gallons water, plus 5 gallons for sparging; 6 pounds German Pilsner malt, 3 pounds Munich malt, 1.5 pounds Caravienne malt**

**60-minute boil: 0.5 ounce Perle hops; 1 ounce Tettnanger hops, divided into halves**

**Ferment: 1 packet German lager yeast, such as Wyeast Oktoberfest; 1 cup honey, for bottling**

- - - - - - - - - - - - - - -

## SUGGESTED FOOD PAIRINGS

- **Grilled meats**
- **Sausages**
- **Roasted vegetables**

# WATCH OUT FOR THIS ONE.

It may be pale in color, but it's not a lightweight. This take on a classic Belgian Tripel clocks in at a hefty 9.9% ABV. This recipe calls for more grain than others in this book, but that makes sense: More grain equals more sugar, which equals more alcohol. We use a base of mostly pilsner malt because it's very efficient at converting starch to fermentable sugar. Saaz hops add a subtle spiciness, while the orange blossom honey leaves a light citrusy tang.

We originally brewed this beer for a special event for the Madewell clothing store in New York City, but we liked it so much we left it on our permanent roster, with an inverted name.

# A WELL-MADE
# TRIPEL
## 9.9% ABV

## 60-MINUTE MASH AT 152°F

3 quarts water, plus 1 gallon for
  sparging
2.8 pounds Belgian Pilsner malt
0.08 pound Caramel 10 malt
*all grains should be milled (see note,
  page 17)

## 60-MINUTE BOIL

0.3 ounce East Kent Golding
  hops
0.1 ounce Saaz hops
0.25 pound clear Belgian
  Candi Sugar (see note,
  page 22)

## FERMENT

½ packet Belgian ale yeast,
  such as Wyeast Belgian
  Abbey 1218 or Safale S-33
  (see note, page 22)
3 tablespoons orange
  blossom honey, for
  bottling

**MASH:** In a medium stockpot, heat the 3 quarts water over high heat to 160°F. Add all the malts and stir gently. The temperature should reduce to 150°F within 1 minute. Turn off the heat. Steep the grains for 60 minutes between 144°F and 152°F. Every 10 minutes, stir and take the temperature. If the grains get too cold, turn on the heat to high while stirring until the temperature rises to that range, then turn off the heat. With 10 minutes left, in a second medium stockpot heat the 1 gallon water to 170°F. After the grains have steeped for 60 minutes, raise the heat of the grains-and-water mixture to high and stir until the temperature reaches 170°F. Turn off the heat.

**SPARGE:** Place a fine-mesh strainer over a pot, and pour the grains into the strainer, reserving the liquid. Pour the 1 gallon of 170°F water over the grains. Recirculate the collected liquid through the grains once.

**BOIL:** Return the pot with the liquid to the stove on high heat and bring to a boil. When it starts to foam, reduce the heat to a slow rolling boil and add the East Kent Golding hops. Add the Saaz hops after 55 minutes. Prepare an ice bath by stopping the sink and filling it with 5 inches of water and ice. At the 60-minute mark, turn off the heat and add the Belgian Candi sugar and stir to dissolve. Place the pot in the ice bath in the sink and cool to 70°F, about 30 minutes.

**FERMENT:** Using a sanitized funnel and strainer, pour the liquid into a sanitized fermenter. Add any water needed to fill the jug to the 1-gallon mark. Add the yeast, sanitize your hands, cover the mouth of the jug with one hand, and shake to distribute evenly. Attach a sanitized stopper and tubing to the fermenter and insert the other end of the tubing into a small bowl of sanitizing solution. The solution will begin to bubble as the yeast activates, pushing gas through the tube. Wait 2 to 3 days until the bubbling has slowed, then replace the tubing system with an airlock (see page 28). Wait 11 more days, then bottle, using the honey (see page 30 for bottling instructions).

**Variation:** Try bottling with other specialty honeys, such as chestnut or lavender.

## FOR 5 GALLONS

**60-minute mash at 152°F: 4 gallons water, plus 5 gallons for sparging; 14 pounds Belgian Pilsner malt, 0.4 pound Caramel 10 malt**

**60-minute boil: 1.5 ounces East Kent Golding hops; 0.5 ounce Saaz hops; 1.25 pounds clear Belgian Candi Sugar**

**Ferment: 1 packet Belgian ale yeast, such as Wyeast Belgian Abbey 1218 or Safale S-33; 1 cup orange blossom honey, for bottling**

- - - - - - - - - - - - - -

## SUGGESTED FOOD PAIRINGS

- **Jerk chicken**
- **Vindaloo**
- **Chili noodles**

# THIS MEDIUM-BODIED ALE

made with a handful of grapes is a nod to harvest season. We like to use super-sweet Concord grapes, which arrive in our markets in September and are like a tarted-up version of supermarket grapes—all heady perfume and juiciness with an almost spicy finish. The malty flavors from the grain are bumped up to bring balance, landing somewhere in the range between an amber and brown ale.

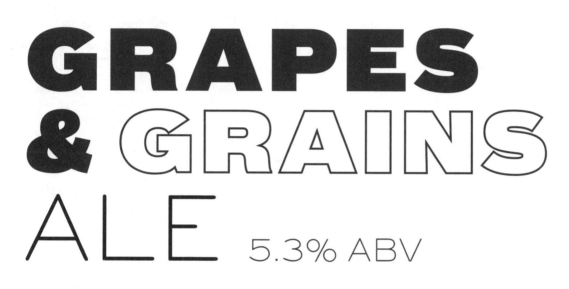

# GRAPES & GRAINS ALE 5.3% ABV

### 60-MINUTE MASH AT 152°F

2 quarts water, plus 1 gallon for sparging

1.6 pounds Belgian Pilsner malt

0.2 pound Caramel 60 malt

0.2 pound Aromatic malt

0.1 pound Cara-pils malt

*all grains should be milled (see note, page 17)

### 60-MINUTE BOIL

0.1 ounce Centennial hops

0.1 ounce Glacier hops

0.01 ounce Whitbread Golding hops

1 cup Concord grapes

### FERMENT

½ packet Belgian ale yeast, such as Safale S-33 (see note, page 22)

3 tablespoons honey, for bottling

**MASH:** In a medium stockpot, heat the 2 quarts water over high heat to 160°F. Add all the malts and stir gently. The temperature should reduce to 150°F within 1 minute. Turn off the heat. Steep the grains for 60 minutes between 144°F and 152°F. Every 10 minutes, stir and take the temperature. If the grains get too cold, turn on the heat to high while stirring until the temperature rises to that range, then turn off the heat. With 10 minutes left, in a second medium stockpot heat the 1 gallon water to 170°F. After the grains have steeped for 60 minutes, raise the heat of the grains-and-water mixture to high and stir until the temperature reaches 170°F. Turn off the heat.

**SPARGE:** Place a fine-mesh strainer over a pot, and pour the grains into the strainer, reserving the liquid. Pour the 1 gallon of 170°F water over the grains. Recirculate the collected liquid through the grains once.

**BOIL:** Return the pot with the liquid to the stove on high heat and bring to a boil. When it starts to foam, reduce the heat to a slow rolling boil and add the Centennial hops. Add the Glacier hops after 30 minutes and the Whitbread Golding hops after 55 minutes. At the 60-minute mark, turn off the heat and add the grapes. Steep for 20 minutes. Prepare an ice bath by stopping the sink and filling it with 5 inches of water and ice. Place the pot in the ice bath in the sink and cool to 70°F, about 20 minutes.

**FERMENT:** Using a sanitized funnel and strainer, pour the liquid into a sanitized fermenter. Add any water needed to fill the jug to the 1-gallon mark. Add the yeast, sanitize your hands, cover the mouth of the jug with one hand, and shake to distribute evenly. Attach a sanitized stopper and tubing to the fermenter and insert the other end of the tubing into a small bowl of sanitizing solution. The solution will begin to bubble as the yeast activates, pushing gas through the tube. Wait 2 to 3 days until the bubbling has slowed, then replace the tubing system with an airlock (see page 28). Wait 11 more days, then bottle, using the honey (see page 30 for bottling instructions).

## FOR 5 GALLONS

**60-minute mash at 152°F: 2½ gallons water, plus 5 gallons for sparging; 8 pounds Belgian Pilsner malt, 1 pound Caramel 60 malt, 1 pound Aromatic malt, 0.5 pound Cara-pils malt**

**60-minute boil: 0.5 ounce Centennial hops; 0.5 ounce Glacier hops; 0.05 ounce Whitbread Golding hops; 5 cups Concord grapes**

**Ferment: 1 packet Belgian ale yeast, such as Safale S-33; 1 cup honey, for bottling**

- - - - - - - - - - - - - - -

## SUGGESTED FOOD PAIRINGS

- **Grilled poultry**
- **Apples**
- **Soft washed-rind cheeses**

# WE WERE INVITED TO BREW BEER

for the NumNum Girls' underground supper club in Brooklyn. Corey Chow, the chef for the night, told us he was going to make something inspired by corned beef and cabbage, but he couldn't get much more specific because he wanted to wait to see what would be in the greenmarkets at the time of the dinner. We came up with this beer. All the flavors of brown ale—the nutty, roasted, malty sweetness—typically pair well with the flavor of mustard, so it makes sense as an addition. This beer has a little kick and a rich, deep spiciness. It turned out to be perfect for Chow's short rib wrapped in cabbage with a dollop of spicy mustard.

# MUSTARD BROWN ALE 6.6% ABV

## 60-MINUTE MASH AT 152°F

2½ quarts water, plus 1 gallon for sparging

1.8 pounds Maris Otter malt

0.2 pound Biscuit malt

0.2 pound Rye malt

0.15 pound Caramel 60 malt

0.1 pound Chocolate malt

*all grains should be milled (see note, page 17)

## 60-MINUTE BOIL

0.16 ounce Chinook hops, divided into halves

0.4 ounce Fuggle hops, divided into halves

5 white peppercorns, crushed

2 tablespoons mustard seeds

## FERMENT

½ packet Belgian ale yeast, such as Safbrew T-58 (see note, page 22)

3 tablespoons honey, for bottling

**MASH:** In a medium stockpot, heat the 2½ quarts water over high heat to 160°F. Add all the malts and stir gently. The temperature should reduce to 150°F within 1 minute. Turn off the heat. Steep the grains for 60 minutes between 144°F and 152°F. Every 10 minutes, stir and take the temperature. If the grains get too cold, turn on the heat to high while stirring until the temperature rises to that range, then turn off the heat. With 10 minutes left, in a second medium stockpot heat the 1 gallon water to 170°F. After the grains have steeped for 60 minutes, raise the heat of the grains-and-water mixture to high and stir until the temperature reaches 170°F. Turn off the heat.

**SPARGE:** Place a fine-mesh strainer over a pot, and pour the grains into the strainer, reserving the liquid. Pour the 1 gallon of 170°F water over the grains. Recirculate the collected liquid through the grains once.

**BOIL:** Return the pot with the liquid to the stove on high heat and bring to a boil. When it starts to foam, reduce the heat to a slow rolling boil and add half of the Chinook hops. Add the remaining Chinook hops after 30 minutes, half of the Fuggle hops and the crushed peppercorns after 45 minutes, the mustard seeds after 50 minutes, and the remaining Fuggle hops after 55 minutes. Prepare an ice bath by stopping the sink and filling it with 5 inches of water and ice. At the 60-minute mark, turn off the heat. Place the pot in the ice bath in the sink and cool to 70°F, about 30 minutes.

**FERMENT:** Using a sanitized funnel and strainer, pour the liquid into a sanitized fermenter. Add any water needed to fill the jug to the 1-gallon mark. Add the yeast, sanitize your hands, cover the mouth of the jug with one hand, and shake to distribute evenly. Attach a sanitized stopper and tubing to the fermenter and insert the other end of the tubing into a small bowl of sanitizing solution. The solution will begin to bubble as the yeast activates, pushing gas through the tube. Wait 2 to 3 days until the bubbling has slowed, then replace the tubing system with an airlock (see page 28). Wait 11 more days, then bottle, using the honey (see page 30 for bottling instructions).

## FOR 5 GALLONS

**60-minute mash at 152°F: 3 gallons water, plus 5 gallons for sparging; 9 pounds Maris Otter malt, 1 pound Biscuit malt, 1 pound Rye malt, 0.75 pound Caramel 60 malt, 0.5 pound Chocolate malt**

**60-minute boil: 0.8 ounce Chinook hops, divided into halves; 2 ounces Fuggle hops, divided into halves; 2 tablespoons white peppercorns, crushed; ½ cup mustard seeds**

**Ferment: 1 packet Belgian ale yeast, such as Safbrew T-58; 1 cup honey, for bottling**

- - - - - - - - - - - - - - -

## SUGGESTED FOOD PAIRINGS

- **Short ribs**
- **Beef stew**
- **Soft pretzels (see page 130)**

**PILGRIMS BREWED BEER** with pumpkins and other winter squash when stores of traditional grains ran low. The pumpkin beers you see on shelves these days use pumpkin more as a flavoring element, and, in some cases, they don't even use the real thing, opting for pumpkin-flavored spice blends instead. In our recipe, roasted pumpkin pulls double duty in this take on a Belgian dubbel (a dark fruity beer). Half the pumpkin goes in with the grains to boost the alcohol content and the other half is added with the hops to get that sweet and rich pumpkin flavor.

Use the same type of small sugar pumpkin that you'd use to make pie. Choose one with lots of ridges, which is a good indication it has more sugar. Smooth pumpkins are more ornamental. If you're feeling inspired, roast a second one as well. You might just have enough downtime while the beer is on the stove to whip up a pie.

# PUMPKIN DUBBEL

7.5% ABV

## PREP

1 sugar pumpkin (1 to 2 pounds)
¼ cup packed light brown sugar

## 60-MINUTE MASH AT 152°F

3 quarts water, plus 1 gallon for
 sparging
2 pounds Belgian Pilsner malt
0.1 pound Belgian Special B malt
0.1 pound Aromatic malt

0.1 pound Caramel 40 malt
0.05 pound Chocolate malt
*all grains should be milled
 (see note, page 17)

## 60-MINUTE BOIL

0.3 ounce Hallertau hops,
 divided into thirds
1 cinnamon stick
5 whole cloves
0.05 ounce Saaz hops

## FERMENT

½ packet Belgian ale yeast,
 such as Safale S-33 (see
 note, page 22)
3 tablespoons maple syrup,
 for bottling

**PREP:** Preheat the oven to 325°F. Peel and seed the pumpkin, cut into 1-inch cubes, and toss in a medium-size bowl with the brown sugar until evenly coated. Place in an oven-safe pan and roast on the bottom rack for 60 minutes, or until soft.

**MASH:** In a medium stockpot, heat the 3 quarts water over high heat to 160°F. Add all the malts and 1 cup of the roasted pumpkin and stir gently. The temperature should reduce to 150°F within 1 minute. Turn off the heat. Steep the grains and pumpkin for 60 minutes between 144°F and 152°F. Every 10 minutes, stir and take the temperature. If the grains and pumpkin get too cold, turn on the heat to high while stirring until the temperature rises to that range, then turn off the heat. With 10 minutes left, in a second medium stockpot heat the 1 gallon water to 170°F. After the grains and pumpkin have steeped for 60 minutes, raise the heat of the grains-pumpkin mixture to high and stir until the temperature reaches 170°F. Turn off the heat.

**SPARGE:** Place a fine-mesh strainer over a pot, and pour the grains and pumpkin into the strainer, reserving the liquid. Pour the 1 gallon of 170°F water over the grains and pumpkin. Recirculate the collected liquid through the grains and pumpkin once.

**BOIL:** Return the pot with the liquid to the stove on high heat and bring to a boil. When it starts to foam, reduce the heat to a slow rolling boil and add two thirds of the Hallertau hops, the cinnamon stick, and

RECIPE CONTINUES

the cloves. Add the remaining 1 cup roasted pumpkin after 30 minutes, the Saaz hops after 45 minutes, and the remaining Hallertau hops after 59 minutes. Prepare an ice bath by stopping the sink and filling it with 5 inches of water and ice. At the 60-minute mark, turn off the heat. Place the pot in the ice bath in the sink and cool to 70°F, about 30 minutes.

**FERMENT:** Using a sanitized funnel and strainer, pour the liquid into a sanitized fermenter. Add any water needed to fill the jug to the 1-gallon mark. Add the yeast, sanitize your hands, cover the mouth of the jug with one hand, and shake to distribute evenly. Attach a sanitized stopper and tubing to the fermenter and insert the other end of the tubing into a small bowl of sanitizing solution. The solution will begin to bubble as the yeast activates, pushing gas through the tube. Wait 2 to 3 days until the bubbling has slowed, then replace the tubing system with an airlock (see page 28). Wait 11 more days, then bottle, using the maple syrup (see page 30 for bottling instructions).

**Variations:** You can use other types of winter squash, such as butternut or acorn, but since they have less sugar than sugar pumpkins, you'll get a slightly less alcoholic beer.

## FOR 5 GALLONS

**Prep:** 3 sugar pumpkins (around 1 to 2 pounds each); 1¼ cups packed light brown sugar

**60-minute mash at 152°F:** 4¼ gallons water, plus 5 gallons for sparging; 10 pounds Belgian Pilsner malt, 0.5 pound Belgian Special B malt, 0.5 pound Aromatic malt, 0.5 pound Caramel 40 malt, 0.25 pound Chocolate malt

**60-minute boil:** 1.5 ounces Hallertau hops, divided into thirds; 3 cinnamon sticks; 2 tablespoons whole cloves; 0.25 ounce Saaz hops

**Ferment:** 1 packet Belgian ale yeast, such as Safale S-33; 1 cup maple syrup, for bottling

- - - - - - - - - - - - - - -

## SUGGESTED FOOD PAIRINGS

- **Mexican moles**
- **Tagines**
- **Pâté**

## A PORTION OF THE FERMENTABLE

sugars in our regular Pumpkin Dubbel (page 124) already comes from roasted pumpkin, so this recipe was a logical choice for a gluten-free beer for fall. To complete the transformation, we dropped the barley entirely and upped the amount of pumpkin, spices, and hops. And to replace the special malt that gives our regular version a raisiny taste, we added some actual raisins.

# GLUTEN-FREE PUMPKIN DUBBEL

3.5% ABV

RECIPE CONTINUES

## PREP

2 pounds whole raw buckwheat (see note, page 93)

1 sugar pumpkin (1 to 2 pounds)

¼ cup packed light brown sugar

## 70-MINUTE MASH

1½ quarts water plus 1½ quarts, plus 1 gallon for sparging

0.2 pound rice hulls (see note, page 61)

## 60-MINUTE BOIL

0.3 ounce Hallertau hops, divided into thirds

3 whole cloves

1 cinnamon stick

½ cup raisins

0.05 ounce Saaz hops

1 cup packed light brown sugar

## FERMENT

½ packet gluten-free yeast, such as Nottingham (see note, page 22)

3 tablespoons maple syrup, for bottling

**PREP:** To malt the buckwheat, rinse the buckwheat, then cover in water and soak for 30 hours, changing the water and rinsing the grains every 8 hours. Strain, rinse once more, then leave the grains in a colander in the dark for 1 day, or until you see the grains begin to sprout. Let the grains sit until the sprouts have doubled in size, about 2 days. Preheat the oven to its lowest setting, or 200°F. Spread the grains over an unoiled rimmed baking sheet and bake for 60 minutes, or until the grains become dry. Rub the dried grains between your hands until the sprouted material falls away. Place the grains in a resealable plastic bag and crush with a rolling pin to "mill."

To roast the pumpkin, preheat the oven to 325°F. Peel and seed the pumpkin, cut into 1-inch cubes, and toss in a medium-size bowl with the brown sugar until evenly coated. Place in an oven-safe pan and roast on the bottom rack for 60 minutes, or until soft.

**MASH:** In a medium stockpot, heat the 1½ quarts water over high heat to 110°F. Add the buckwheat and stir gently. The temperature should drop to 95°F. Turn off the heat. Steep the grains for 15 minutes at 95°F, then turn the heat on high while stirring to raise the temperature to 113°F. Turn off the heat. Steep the grains for 15 minutes at 113°F, then add the rice hulls, an additional 1½ quarts water, and 1 cup of the roasted pumpkin and turn the heat on high while stirring to raise the temperature to 149°F. Steep the grains-pumpkin mixture for 40 minutes at 149°F. Every 10 minutes, stir and take the temperature. If the grains-pumpkin mixture gets too cold, turn on the heat to high while stirring until the temperature rises to 149°F, then turn off the heat. With 10 minutes left, in a second medium stockpot heat the 1 gallon of water to 150°F.

**SPARGE:** Place a fine-mesh strainer over a pot, and pour the grains and pumpkin into the strainer, reserving the liquid. Pour the 1 gallon of 150°F water over the grains and pumpkin. Recirculate the collected liquid through the grains and pumpkin once.

**BOIL:** Return the pot with the liquid to the stove on high heat and bring to a boil. When it starts to foam, reduce the heat to a slow rolling boil and add two thirds of the Hallertau hops, the cloves, and the cinnamon stick. Add the remaining 1 cup roasted pumpkin and the raisins after 30 minutes, the Saaz hops after 45 minutes, and the remaining Hallertau hops after 59 minutes. Prepare an ice bath by stopping the sink and filling it with 5 inches of water and ice. At the 60-minute mark, turn off the heat, add the sugar, and stir to dissolve. Place the pot in the ice bath in the sink and cool to 70°F, about 30 minutes.

**FERMENT:** Using a sanitized funnel and strainer, pour the liquid into a sanitized fermenter. Add any water needed to fill the jug to the 1-gallon mark. Add the gluten-free yeast, sanitize your hands, cover the mouth of the jug with one hand, and shake to distribute evenly. Attach a sanitized stopper and tubing to the fermenter and insert the other end of the tubing into a small bowl of sanitizing solution. The solution will begin to bubble as the yeast activates, pushing gas through the tube. Wait 2 to 3 days until the bubbling has slowed, then replace the tubing system with an airlock (see page 28). Wait 11 more days, then bottle, using the maple syrup (see page 30 for bottling instructions).

## FOR 5 GALLONS

**Prep: 3 sugar pumpkins (1 to 2 pounds each); 1¼ cups packed light brown sugar**

**70-minute mash: 2½ gallons water, plus 5 gallons for sparging; 10 pounds malted buckwheat, 0.5 pound rice hulls**

**60-minute boil: 1.5 ounces Hallertau hops, divided into thirds; 2 tablespoons whole cloves; 3 cinnamon sticks; 2½ cups raisins; 0.25 ounce Saaz hops; 5 cups packed light brown sugar**

**Ferment: 1 packet gluten-free yeast, such as Nottingham; 1 cup maple syrup, for bottling**

## SUGGESTED FOOD PAIRINGS

- **Stews**
- **Chili**
- **Roasted lamb**

# BEER-BOILED
# PRETZEL BITES

We perfected these bite-size pretzels for Erica's Oktoberfest-themed birthday party a few years ago. We went all out—30 pounds of hand-made sausage, 5 kegs of beer—and had a grand plan to shape, boil, and bake authentic pretzels to order for each guest. Turns out, twisting pretzels is not as easy as it looks, and so we ended up making them in this much less fussy shape. They get just a hint of flavor from the beer and work especially well with our Beer Mustard (page 132).

**SERVES 6 to 8**

2 cups warm water (about 110°F)

1 package active dry yeast

¼ cup packed light brown sugar

5 cups all-purpose flour, plus more for surface

2½ teaspoons kosher salt, plus more for sprinkling

¼ pound (1 stick) unsalted butter, cubed and chilled

Vegetable oil

8 cups water

½ cup baking soda

½ cup beer, such as Mustard Brown Ale (page 122), Oktoberfest (page 116), or Rye P.A. (page 104)

1 egg, lightly beaten

- - - - - - - - - - - - - - - - - - - - - - - - - - - - - - - - - - - - - - - - - - - - -

Place the warm water, yeast, and a pinch of the brown sugar in a small bowl and stir to dissolve. Let the mixture stand for 5 minutes, or until it develops a light foam. In a large bowl, stir together the flour and salt. Add the butter cubes and continue to mix with your hands until the mixture is crumbly. Add the yeast mixture and fold with your hands until a shaggy dough is formed and the liquid is absorbed, then knead until the dough is smooth and begins to pull away from the side of the bowl, about 5 minutes.

Transfer the dough to a floured surface and continue to knead with your hands until the ball is smooth and elastic, about 10 minutes. Place the dough ball into an oiled medium-size bowl, cover with a damp cloth, and leave in a warm spot until the dough has doubled in size, about 1 hour.

Preheat the oven to 450°F. On a floured surface, roll the dough out into a large square (about 12 × 12 inches). Using an oiled knife, cut the dough into 12 one-inch strips. Using your hands, roll each strip into a rope until it doubles in length, about 24 inches. Using kitchen shears or a knife, cut the strips into 1-inch pieces.

In a large saucepan, combine the 8 cups water, the baking soda, beer, and the remaining brown sugar over high heat, stirring to dissolve the sugar. When the liquid reaches a boil, reduce the heat to a simmer. Using a slotted spoon, place the pretzel pieces in the simmering liquid and cook until the bites float, about 30 seconds. Transfer the boiled bites to a lightly oiled baking sheet using the slotted spoon. Brush the bites with the beaten egg and sprinkle with salt.

Bake for 5 minutes on the lowest rack, then rotate the baking sheet and continue baking until the bites turn a chestnut brown color, about 5 minutes more. Remove from the oven and place the bites on a wire rack to cool. The pretzels are best when consumed right away, but they can be stored in an airtight container for up to 2 days.

# BEER MUSTARD

Beer makes a great addition to mustard. The sweet edge to the beer helps ground the sharpness. This mustard is perfect for using in poultry and ham dishes, or try serving it with our Beer-Boiled Pretzel Bites (page 130) for a real crowd-pleaser.

**MAKES 2 cups**

¾ cup mustard seeds

2 teaspoons crushed turmeric seeds

12 tablespoons beer, such as Mustard Brown Ale (page 122), Imperial Pepper Stout (page 108), or Prohibition Ale (page 106)

2 tablespoons olive oil

2 shallots, diced

1 teaspoon salt

2 tablespoons white wine vinegar

- - - - - - - - - - - - - - - - - - - - - - - - - - - - - - - - - - - - - - - - - - - - - - - - - - -

Cover the mustard seeds in a bowl in cold water and soak for 3 hours. Using a cheesecloth over a fine-mesh strainer, strain the mustard seeds. Pulse the wet mustard seeds, turmeric seeds, and beer in a food processor until combined, or grind together with a mortar and pestle. In a medium-size skillet, heat the olive oil over medium heat. Add the shallots and cook until caramelized, about 5 minutes. Add the caramelized shallots and the salt to the mustard-beer mixture. Stir in the vinegar, then transfer the mustard to a nonreactive airtight container and refrigerate for at least 4 hours before using. Use within 2 weeks.

# MALTED APPLE
# ICE CREAM

**NOTE:** YOU'LL NEED AN ICE CREAM MAKER FOR THIS RECIPE.

This is a delicious way to use the malted apples left over from brewing the Apple Crisp Ale.

**MAKES 2 quarts**

2 cooked apples from the Apple Crisp Ale (page 102), or 2 baked apples, sliced

2 tablespoons packed light brown sugar

Vegetable oil

2 cups whole milk

1 cinnamon stick

6 egg yolks

½ cup granulated sugar

¼ teaspoon molasses

Pinch of salt

1 cup heavy cream

- - - - - - - - - - - - - - - - - - - - - - - - - - - - - - - - - - - - - - - - - - - - - -

Preheat the oven to 350°F. In a medium bowl, toss the apples in the brown sugar to coat. On a lightly oiled baking sheet, bake the apples on the lowest rack of the oven for 20 minutes, or until golden brown. Set aside to cool.

In a medium saucepan, heat the milk over medium-high heat until it boils. Add the cinnamon stick, turn off the heat, and steep for 20 minutes, uncovered. In a medium bowl, whisk together the egg yolks, granulated sugar, molasses, and the pinch of salt.

Remove the cinnamon stick from the milk and bring the milk back to a boil over medium-high heat. Whisk about ½ cup of the hot milk into the egg mixture, then pour the egg-milk mixture into the remaining boiling milk, whisking constantly. Turn the heat to low and stir until the mixture thickens enough to coat the back of a spoon. Remove from the heat and stir in the heavy cream. Cover the custard with plastic wrap and refrigerate until cool. Pour custard into your ice cream machine, and follow the manufacturer's instructions. After the custard thickens, stir in the apples.

# WINTER

## WINTER IS THE PERFECT TIME FOR BREWING. It's dark outside and nice to have the stove on, plus there is a string of holiday parties to make beer for. Warming stouts and porters are good beers for this season, making use of the spices found in baked goods or herbs usually reserved for winter roasts.

The roster of drinks associated with the winter holidays—eggnog, mulled wine, warmed cider, spiked hot chocolate, and Champagne—also serve as great inspiration. We've come up with some great riffs: our own take on eggnog wrapped up in a milk stout, gingerbread beer for dipping cookies, and even a classic bubbly Belgian beer for ringing in the New Year. Give the punch bowl a rest: Brew them by the gallon for a more private toast or make them in five-gallon batches for a celebration.

CHOCOLATE MAPLE PORTER

------

CHESTNUT BROWN ALE

------

GINGERBREAD ALE

------

HONEY SAGE SEASONAL

------

ROSEMARY SCOTCH ALE

------

O TANNENBOCK SPRUCE ALE

------

BOURBON DUBBEL

------

WINTER WHEAT

------

COFFEE & DONUT STOUT

------

DATES & HONEY ALE

------

NEW YEAR BEER

------

EGGNOG MILK STOUT

------

GLUTEN-FREE GINGERBREAD ALE

------

BEER & CARAMEL POPCORN • BEER & SAGE FONDUE

------

BEER ICE CREAM FLOAT • SPENT-GRAIN DOG BISCUITS

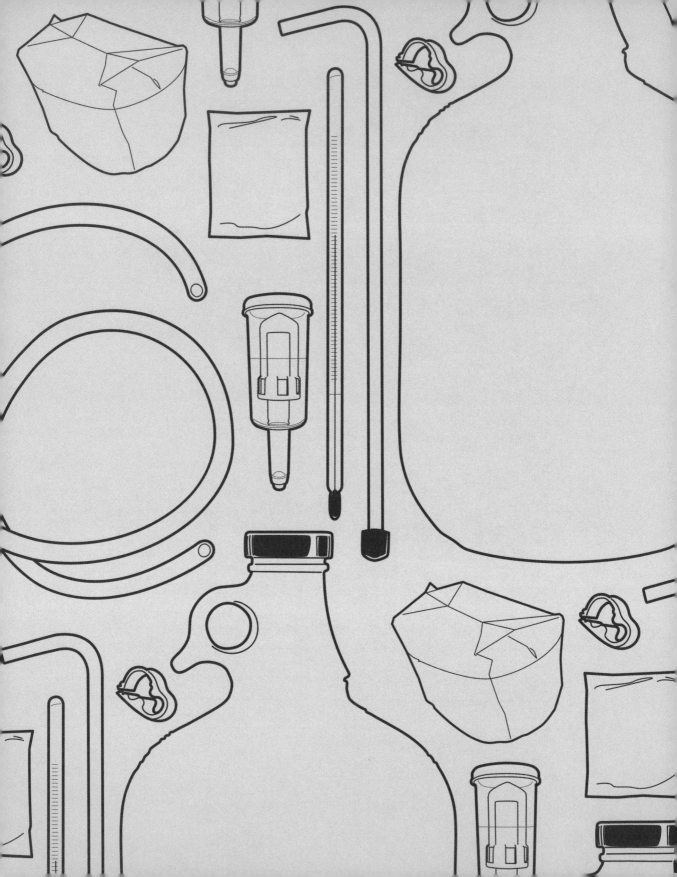

# WINTER FEATURE

The holiday season is our busiest time of year, with kits and mixes flying out of the warehouse for gifts. We like the idea of making beer as presents, too. You'll need to start at least two weeks ahead of time (or four if you want the recipient to be able to drink it right away), so plan accordingly. Here are some tips:

- Get a few nice bottles and spend some time making clever labels while the beer is on the stove. Use high-quality paper and handsome ribbons to tie a label around each bottle.

- Pair a few bottles with a bag of the Beer & Caramel Popcorn (page 166), Beer Mustard (page 132), or Lavender Shortbread (page 63) for a well-rounded package. Or make beer for your favorite dog owners and use the spent grain to make Spent-Grain Dog Biscuits (page 169) for their pup.

- A six-pack sampler of different beers you've made can be fun. You can paste cardstock over regular six-pack holders to personalize them.

- Give beer and a beer kit, with the promise of brewing together in the future.

## AGING BEERS

The general rule of thumb is the lighter the beer, the earlier you want to drink it, and likewise those with fresh hop flavor, such as I.P.A.s. Darker beers or those with more alcohol, such as the Imperial Pepper Stout (page 108) and the Bourbon Dubbel (page 150), can be aged up to two years with great success. The fresh fruity flavors will mellow into something more tart and complicated. Store bottles upright in a cool, dark place. Try a bottle along the way to see how the beer is developing.

# IF YOU LIKE THE RICH ROASTED FLAVOR OF DARK BEERS, you'll love this take

on a classic dark English porter. We have sold it at the Brooklyn Flea since day one. The dark chocolate flavor actually comes from a handful of Chocolate malt, a super-dark roast of barley. Maple syrup added at the end of the boil makes the body smooth and creamy, and an English-style yeast tops it off with a frothy tan head.

# CHOCOLATE MAPLE PORTER
## 6.5% ABV

### 60-MINUTE MASH AT 152°F

2 quarts water, plus 1 gallon for sparging

1.2 pounds American 2-row malt

0.3 pound Chocolate malt

0.2 pound Caramel 15 malt

0.2 pound Black Patent malt

*all grains should be milled (see note, page 17)

### 60-MINUTE BOIL

0.4 ounce Fuggle hops, divided into quarters

¾ cup maple syrup

### FERMENT

½ packet English ale yeast, such as Nottingham or Wyeast London III (see note, page 22)

3 tablespoons maple syrup, for bottling

**MASH:** In a medium stockpot, heat the 2 quarts water over high heat to 160°F. Add all the malts and stir gently. The temperature should reduce to 150°F within 1 minute. Turn off the heat. Steep the grains for 60 minutes between 144°F and 152°F. Every 10 minutes, stir and take the temperature. If the grains get too cold, turn on the heat to high while stirring until the temperature rises to that range, then turn off the heat. With 10 minutes left, in a second medium stockpot heat the 1 gallon water to 170°F. After the grains have steeped for 60 minutes, raise the heat of the grains-and-water mixture to high and stir until the temperature reaches 170°F. Turn off the heat.

**SPARGE:** Place a fine-mesh strainer over a pot, and pour the grains into the strainer, reserving the liquid. Pour the 1 gallon of 170°F water over the grains. Recirculate the collected liquid through the grains once.

**BOIL:** Return the pot with the liquid to the stove on high heat and bring to a boil. When it starts to foam, reduce the heat to a slow rolling boil and add three quarters of the Fuggle hops. Add the remaining hops after 45 minutes. Prepare an ice bath by stopping the sink and filling it with 5 inches of water and ice. At the 60-minute mark, turn off the heat, add the ¾ cup maple syrup, and stir to dissolve. Place the pot in the ice bath in the sink and cool to 70°F, about 30 minutes.

**FERMENT:** Using a sanitized funnel and strainer, pour the liquid into a sanitized fermenter. Add any water needed to fill the jug to the 1-gallon mark. Add the yeast, sanitize your hands, cover the mouth of the jug with one hand, and shake to distribute evenly. Attach a sanitized stopper and tubing to the fermenter and insert the other end of the tubing into a small bowl of sanitizing solution. The solution will begin to bubble as the yeast activates, pushing gas through the tube. Wait 2 to 3 days until the bubbling has slowed, then replace the tubing system with an airlock (see page 28). Wait 11 more days, then bottle, using the 3 tablespoons maple syrup (see page 30 for bottling instructions).

## FOR 5 GALLONS

**60-minute mash at 152°F: 2.5 gallons water, plus 5 gallons for sparging; 6 pounds American 2-row malt, 1.5 pounds Chocolate malt, 1 pound Caramel 15 malt, 1 pound Black Patent malt**

**60-minute boil: 2 ounces Fuggle hops, divided into quarters; 3¾ cups maple syrup**

**Ferment: 1 packet English ale yeast, such as Nottingham or Wyeast London III; 1 cup maple syrup, for bottling**

## SUGGESTED FOOD PAIRINGS
- **Pulled pork**
- **Blue cheese**
- **Roasted beets**

**NORTHERN ENGLISH BROWN ALES ALREADY HAVE NOTES OF CARAMEL AND NUTS;** the flavor comes from the roasted malts typically used in that style. Here, adding chestnuts to the boil amplifies the nuttiness, creating a sweet, mellow, satisfying flavor. Brewing with chestnuts is more common in France and Italy, where the soft nut shows up in culinary specialties like pastas, gratins, and salads. The fat content of most nuts will make beer spoil; chestnuts, with their low fat content, are the exception. Roast some extra chestnuts for a snack.

# CHESTNUT BROWN ALE 6.0% ABV

**PREP**

3 chestnuts

**60-MINUTE MASH AT 152°F**

2 quarts water, plus 1 gallon for sparging
1.5 pounds Maris Otter malt
0.2 pound Caramel 60 malt
0.2 pound Caramel 120 malt
0.02 pound roasted barley
*all grains should be milled (see note, page 17)

**60-MINUTE BOIL**

0.3 ounce East Kent Golding hops, divided into thirds

**FERMENT**

½ packet English ale yeast, such as Safale S-04 (see note, page 22)
3 tablespoons honey, for bottling

**PREP:** Preheat the oven to 400°F. Cut a small crosshatch into each chestnut shell. Roast on a baking sheet for 20 minutes, or until the shells have peeled back. Remove from the oven and cover. After 10 minutes, peel off the shells, reserving the nuts.

**MASH:** In a medium stockpot, heat the 2 quarts water over high heat to 160°F. Add all the malts and barley and stir gently. The temperature should reduce to 150°F within 1 minute. Turn off the heat. Steep the grains for 60 minutes between 144°F and 152°F. Every 10 minutes, stir and take the temperature. If the grains get too cold, turn on the heat to high while stirring until the temperature rises to that range, then turn off the heat. With 10 minutes left, in a second medium stockpot heat the 1 gallon water to 170°F. After the grains have steeped for 60 minutes, raise the heat of the grains-and-water mixture to high and stir until the temperature reaches 170°F. Turn off the heat.

**SPARGE:** Place a fine-mesh strainer over a pot, and pour the grains into the strainer, reserving the liquid. Pour the 1 gallon of 170°F water over the grains. Recirculate the collected liquid through the grains once.

**BOIL:** Return the pot with the liquid to the stove on high heat and bring to a boil. When it starts to foam, reduce the heat to a slow rolling boil and add two thirds of the East Kent Golding hops and the roasted and peeled chestnuts. Add the remainder of the hops after 40 minutes. Prepare an ice bath by stopping the sink and filling it with 5 inches of water and ice. At the 60-minute mark, turn off the heat. Place the pot in the ice bath in the sink and cool to 70°F, about 30 minutes.

**FERMENT:** Using a sanitized funnel and strainer, pour the liquid into a sanitized fermenter. Add any water needed to fill the jug to the 1-gallon mark. Add the yeast, sanitize your hands, cover the mouth of the jug with one hand, and shake to distribute evenly. Attach a sanitized stopper and tubing to the fermenter and insert the other end of the tubing into a small bowl of sanitizing solution. The solution will begin to bubble as the yeast activates, pushing gas through the tube. Wait 2 to 3 days until the bubbling has slowed, then replace the tubing system with an airlock (see page 28). Wait 11 more days, then bottle, using the honey (see page 30 for bottling instructions).

## FOR 5 GALLONS

**Prep: 15 chestnuts**

**60-minute mash at 152°F: 2½ gallons water, plus 5 gallons for sparging; 7.5 pounds Maris Otter malt, 1 pound Caramel 60 malt, 1 pound Caramel 120 malt, 0.1 pound roasted barley**

**60-minute boil: 1.5 ounces East Kent Golding hops, divided into thirds**

**Ferment: 1 packet English ale yeast, such as Safale S-04; 1 cup honey, for bottling**

- - - - - - - - - - - - - - - -

## SUGGESTED FOOD PAIRINGS

· **Roasted chicken**
· **Root vegetables**
· **Gratin**

# A GINGERBREAD RECIPE FROM NEW YORK CITY'S GRAMERCY TAVERN

gave us the inspiration for this spiced winter warmer. Candied ginger is our secret weapon. It dissolves, leaving that familiar mellow ginger flavor found in the best cookies. Whole cloves, a stick of cinnamon, and fresh gratings of nutmeg round out the spice mix and impart a cozy room-filling aroma both on the stove while cooking and, later, in the glass while drinking.

# GINGER-BREAD ALE 6.5% ABV

## 60-MINUTE MASH AT 152°F

- 2½ quarts water, plus 1 gallon for sparging
- 1.8 pounds English Pale malt
- 0.2 pound Caramel 10 malt
- 0.2 pound Caramel 60 malt
- 0.1 pound Chocolate malt
- *all grains should be milled (see note, page 17)

## 60-MINUTE BOIL

- 0.2 ounce Centennial hops
- 1 cinnamon stick
- 3 whole cloves
- 1 teaspoon candied ginger
- ½ whole nutmeg, grated
- 0.1 ounce Hallertau hops

## FERMENT

- ½ packet English ale yeast, such as Nottingham (see note, page 22)
- 3 tablespoons honey, for bottling

**MASH:** In a medium stockpot, heat the 2½ quarts water over high heat to 160°F. Add all the malts and stir gently. The temperature should reduce to 150°F within 1 minute. Turn off the heat. Steep the grains for 60 minutes between 144°F and 152°F. Every 10 minutes, stir and take the temperature. If the grains get too cold, turn on the heat to high while stirring until the temperature rises to that range, then turn off the heat. With 10 minutes left, in a second medium stockpot heat the 1 gallon water to 170°F. After the grains have steeped for 60 minutes, raise the heat of the grains-and-water mixture to high and stir until the temperature reaches 170°F. Turn off the heat.

**SPARGE:** Place a fine-mesh strainer over a pot, and pour the grains into the strainer, reserving the liquid. Pour the 1 gallon of 170°F water over the grains. Recirculate the collected liquid through the grains once.

**BOIL:** Return the pot with the liquid to the stove on high heat and bring to a boil. When it starts to foam, reduce the heat to a slow rolling boil and add the Centennial hops, cinnamon stick, and cloves. Add the candied ginger and nutmeg after 30 minutes and the Hallertau hops after 55 minutes. Prepare an ice bath by stopping the sink and filling it with 5 inches of water and ice. At the 60-minute mark, turn off the heat. Place the pot in the ice bath in the sink and cool to 70°F, about 30 minutes.

**FERMENT:** Using a sanitized funnel and strainer, pour the liquid into a sanitized fermenter. Add any water needed to fill the jug to the 1-gallon mark. Add the yeast, sanitize your hands, cover the mouth of the jug with one hand, and shake to distribute evenly. Attach a sanitized stopper and tubing to the fermenter and insert the other end of the tubing into a small bowl of sanitizing solution. The solution will begin to bubble as the yeast activates, pushing gas through the tube. Wait 2 to 3 days until the bubbling has slowed, then replace the tubing system with an airlock (see page 28). Wait 11 more days, then bottle, using the honey (see page 30 for bottling instructions).

## FOR 5 GALLONS

**60-minute mash at 152°F: 3 gallons water, plus 5 gallons for sparging; 9 pounds English Pale malt, 1 pound Caramel 10 malt, 1 pound Caramel 60 malt, 0.5 pound Chocolate malt**

**60-minute boil: 1 ounce Centennial hops; 4 cinnamon sticks; 12 whole cloves; 2 tablespoons candied ginger; 2 whole nutmegs, grated; 0.5 ounce Hallertau hops**

**Ferment: 1 packet English ale yeast, such as Nottingham; 1 cup honey, for bottling**

- - - - - - - - - - - - - - -

## SUGGESTED FOOD PAIRINGS

· **Vanilla ice cream**
· **Pumpkin pie**
· **Gingersnaps**

# WE ORIGINALLY BREWED THIS AS A LIGHT SUMMER BEER,

but sage—the signature of hearty stuffings, sausages, and pastas—really belongs in the winter line-up. The key to brewing with sage is restraint: add too much and the beer will take on a resinous, almost medicinal quality. Here, the chopped leaves are added in the final stages for just a hint of savory aromatics that resonates with the earthiness of Styrian Golding hops. Honey rounds out the herbal notes and adds a lushness to the body.

# HONEY SAGE SEASONAL

## 7.1% ABV

### 60-MINUTE MASH AT 152°F

2¼ quarts water, plus 1 gallon for sparging

1.8 pounds Belgian Pilsner malt

0.3 pound Munich malt

*all grains should be milled (see note, page 17)

### 60-MINUTE BOIL

0.3 ounce Styrian Golding hops, divided into thirds

3 tablespoons chopped fresh sage

0.2 pound clear Belgian Candi Sugar (see note, page 22)

¾ cup honey

### FERMENT

½ packet Belgian ale yeast, such as Safale T-58 (see note, page 22)

3 tablespoons honey, for bottling

**MASH:** In a medium stockpot, heat the 2¼ quarts water over high heat to 160°F. Add all the malts and stir gently. The temperature should reduce to 150°F within 1 minute. Turn off the heat. Steep the grains for 60 minutes between 144°F and 152°F. Every 10 minutes, stir and take the temperature. If the grains get too cold, turn on the heat to high while stirring until the temperature rises to that range, then turn off the heat. With 10 minutes left, in a second medium stockpot heat the 1 gallon water to 170°F. After the grains have steeped for 60 minutes, raise the heat of the grains-and-water mixture to high and stir until the temperature reaches 170°F. Turn off the heat.

**SPARGE:** Place a fine-mesh strainer over a pot, and pour the grains into the strainer, reserving the liquid. Pour the 1 gallon of 170°F water over the grains. Recirculate the collected liquid through the grains once.

**BOIL:** Return the pot with the liquid to the stove on high heat and bring to a boil. When it starts to foam, reduce the heat to a slow rolling boil and add one third of the Styrian Golding hops. Add another third of the hops after 30 minutes, 2 tablespoons of the sage after 50 minutes, and the remaining hops after 55 minutes. Prepare an ice bath by stopping the sink and filling it with 5 inches of water and ice. At the 60-minute mark, turn off the heat, add the remaining sage, the Belgian Candi Sugar, and the ¾ cup honey, and stir to dissolve. Place the pot in the ice bath in the sink and cool to 70°F, about 30 minutes.

**FERMENT:** Using a sanitized funnel and strainer, pour the liquid into a sanitized fermenter. Add any water needed to fill the jug to the 1-gallon mark. Add the yeast, sanitize your hands, cover the mouth of the jug with one hand, and shake to distribute evenly. Attach a sanitized stopper and tubing to the fermenter and insert the other end of the tubing into a small bowl of sanitizing solution. The solution will begin to bubble as the yeast activates, pushing gas through the tube. Wait 2 to 3 days until the bubbling has slowed, then replace the tubing system with an airlock (see page 28). Wait 11 more days, then bottle, using the 3 tablespoons honey (see page 30 for bottling instructions).

## FOR 5 GALLONS

**60-minute mash at 152°F: 3 gallons water, plus 5 gallons for sparging; 9 pounds Belgian Pilsner malt, 1.5 pounds Munich malt**

**60-minute boil: 1.5 ounces Styrian Golding hops, divided into thirds; 1 cup chopped fresh sage; 1 pound clear Belgian Candi Sugar; 3¾ cups honey**

**Ferment: 1 packet Belgian ale yeast, such as Safale T-58; 1 cup honey, for bottling**

- - - - - - - - - - - - - - - -

## SUGGESTED FOOD PAIRINGS

- **Roasted winter squash**
- **Poultry sausages**
- **Hard sheep's-milk cheese**

# WE LIKE TO KEEP A POTTED ROSEMARY PLANT GOING YEAR-ROUND IN OUR KITCHEN GARDEN.

The clean, cutting, almost camphorous flavor provides the perfect accent to cold-weather favorites like roasted red potatoes, grilled steak, and minestrone soup. In this beer, the herb's vibrant notes of pine and citrus complement a typical Scotch Ale base. Golden Promise is a Scottish malt that is similar to Maris Otter, while Melanoidin malt leaves a rich red color and a strong malty flavor.

# ROSEMARY SCOTCH ALE 8.8% ABV

## 60-MINUTE MASH AT 152°F

- 3½ quarts water, plus 1 gallon for sparging
- 2.2 pounds Golden Promise malt
- 0.4 pound Peat Smoked malt
- 0.3 pound Melanoidin malt
- 0.3 pound Caramel 60 malt
- 0.1 pound Cara-pils malt
- 0.04 pound roasted barley
- *all grains should be milled (see note, page 17)

## 75-MINUTE BOIL

- 0.2 ounce East Kent Golding hops, divided into halves
- 0.1 ounce Brambling Cross hops
- 2 sprigs of rosemary, divided use
- 0.04 ounce Whitbread Golding hops

## FERMENT

- ½ packet Scottish ale yeast, such as Wyeast Edinburgh (see note, page 22)
- 3 tablespoons maple syrup, for bottling

**MASH:** In a medium stockpot, heat the 3½ quarts water over high heat to 160°F. Add all the malts and barley and stir gently. The temperature should reduce to 150°F within 1 minute. Turn off the heat. Steep the grains for 60 minutes between 144°F and 152°F. Every 10 minutes, stir and take the temperature. If the grains get too cold, turn on the heat to high while stirring until the temperature rises to that range, then turn off the heat. With 10 minutes left, in a second medium stockpot heat the 1 gallon water to 170°F. After the grains have steeped for 60 minutes, raise the heat of the grains-and-water mixture to high and stir until the temperature reaches 170°F. Turn off the heat.

**SPARGE:** Place a fine-mesh strainer over a pot, and pour the grains into the strainer, reserving the liquid. Pour the 1 gallon of 170°F water over the grains. Recirculate the collected liquid through the grains once.

**BOIL:** Return the pot with the liquid to the stove on high heat and bring to a boil. When it starts to foam, reduce the heat to a slow rolling boil and add half of the East Kent Golding hops after 15 minutes, the remaining East Kent Golding hops after 30 minutes, the Brambling Cross hops after 45 minutes, 1 sprig of rosemary after 60 minutes, and the Whitbread Golding hops and remaining rosemary after 70 minutes. Prepare an ice bath by stopping the sink and filling it with 5 inches of water and ice. At the 75-minute mark, turn off the heat. Place the pot in the ice bath in the sink and cool to 70°F, about 30 minutes.

**FERMENT:** Using a sanitized funnel and strainer, pour the liquid into a sanitized fermenter. Add any water needed to fill the jug to the 1-gallon mark. Add the yeast, sanitize your hands, cover the mouth of the jug with one hand, and shake to distribute evenly. Attach a sanitized stopper and tubing to the fermenter and insert the other end of the tubing into a small bowl of sanitizing solution. The solution will begin to bubble as the yeast activates, pushing gas through the tube. Wait 2 to 3 days until the bubbling has slowed, then replace the tubing system with an airlock (see page 28). Wait 11 more days, then bottle, using the maple syrup (see page 30 for bottling instructions).

## FOR 5 GALLONS

**60-minute mash at 152°F: 4½ gallons water, plus 5 gallons for sparging; 11 pounds Golden Promise malt, 2 pounds Peat Smoked malt, 1.5 pounds Melanoidin malt, 1.5 pounds Caramel 60 malt, 0.5 pound Cara-pils malt, 0.2 pound roasted barley**

**75-minute boil: 1 ounce East Kent Golding hops, divided into halves; 0.5 ounce Brambling Cross hops; 6 sprigs of rosemary; 0.2 ounce Whitbread Golding hops**

**Ferment: 1 packet Scottish ale yeast, such as Wyeast Edinburgh; 1 cup maple syrup, for bottling**

– – – – – – – – – – – – – –

## SUGGESTED FOOD PAIRINGS

- **Roasted beef**
- **Lamb**
- **Root vegetables**

# THIS DARK, PINEY BEER IS INSPIRED BY BEN FRANKLIN,

who, like Thomas Jefferson, George Washington, and many others in colonial America, brewed beer at home. One recipe reportedly shows him using molasses and spruce. There is something invigorating about the idea of brewing a beer with spruce. The aromatics seem healthy and fresh, as though you've just had a snowball fight in a forest. Unless you have a spruce tree in your backyard, it can be tricky to find the right materials. Wait until December, when cut trees arrive in parking lots, on street corners, and in tents outside supermarkets. A clipping off your (or your neighbor's) Christmas tree will be perfect.

# O TANNENBOCK SPRUCE ALE 5.7% ABV

## 60-MINUTE MASH AT 152°F

1¾ quarts water, plus 1 gallon for sparging

1.5 pounds Pale Ale malt

0.1 pound Cara-pils malt

0.2 pound flaked barley

*all grains should be milled (see note, page 17)

## 60-MINUTE BOIL

0.12 ounce Chinook hops, divided into halves

0.04 ounce Simcoe hops

1 six-inch long sprig of spruce

½ cup molasses

## FERMENT

½ packet English ale yeast, such as Safale S-04 (see note, page 22)

3 tablespoons maple syrup, for bottling

**MASH:** In a medium stockpot, heat the 1¾ quarts water over high heat to 160°F. Add all the malts and barley and stir gently. The temperature should reduce to 150°F within 1 minute. Turn off the heat. Steep the grains for 60 minutes between 144°F and 152°F. Every 10 minutes, stir and take the temperature. If the grains get too cold, turn on the heat to high while stirring until the temperature rises to that range, then turn off the heat. With 10 minutes left, in a second medium stockpot heat 1 gallon water to 170°F. After the grains have steeped for 60 minutes, raise the heat of the grains-and-water mixture to high and stir until the temperature reaches 170°F. Turn off the heat.

**SPARGE:** Place a fine-mesh strainer over a pot, and pour the grains into the strainer, reserving the liquid. Pour the 1 gallon of 170°F water over the grains. Recirculate the collected liquid through the grains once.

**BOIL:** Return the pot with the liquid to the stove on high heat and bring to a boil. When it starts to foam, reduce the heat to a slow rolling boil and add half of the Chinook hops. Add the remaining Chinook hops after 30 minutes, the Simcoe hops after 50 minutes, and the spruce sprig after 55 minutes. Prepare an ice bath by stopping the sink and filling it with 5 inches of water and ice. At the 60-minute mark, turn off the heat, add the molasses, and stir to dissolve. Place the pot in the ice bath in the sink and cool to 70°F, about 30 minutes.

**FERMENT:** Using a sanitized funnel and strainer, pour the liquid into a sanitized fermenter. Add any water needed to fill the jug to the 1-gallon mark. Add the yeast, sanitize your hands, cover the mouth of the jug with one hand, and shake to distribute evenly. Attach a sanitized stopper and tubing to the fermenter and insert the other end of the tubing into a small bowl of sanitizing solution. The solution will begin to bubble as the yeast activates, pushing gas through the tube. Wait 2 to 3 days until the bubbling has slowed, then replace the tubing system with an airlock (see page 28). Wait 11 more days, then bottle, using the maple syrup (see page 30 for bottling instructions).

## FOR 5 GALLONS

**60-minute mash at 152°F:**
2¼ gallons water, plus 5 gallons for sparging; 7.5 pounds Pale Ale malt, 0.5 pound Cara-pils malt, 1 pound flaked barley

**60-minute boil:**
0.6 ounce Chinook hops, divided into halves; 0.2 ounce Simcoe hops; 3 six-inch spruce sprigs; 2½ cups molasses

**Ferment:** 1 packet English ale yeast, such as Safale S-04; 1 cup maple syrup, for bottling

- - - - - - - - - - - - - -

## SUGGESTED FOOD PAIRINGS

· **Grilled wild meats**
· **Roasted game birds**
· **Sheep's-milk cheeses**

**WE LOVE THE VANILLA AND SMOKY CHARRED NOTES BOURBON GETS FROM AGING IN OAK BARRELS.** To get the same effect in small-batch beer, we soak dark oak chips in bourbon overnight, then add them to the boil. Most commercial bourbon beers are super-heavy stouts that can knock you out after the first sip, but we chose a lighter style of Belgian dubbel for the base, more spice and plum than syrup.

# BOURBON DUBBEL

## 7.0% ABV

### PREP

0.75 ounce dark oak chips (available at brewing supply stores, see Sources, page 172)

⅓ cup bourbon

### 60-MINUTE MASH AT 152°F

2¼ quarts water, plus 1 gallon for sparging

1.7 pounds Belgian Pilsner malt

0.25 pound Munich malt

0.2 pound Special B malt

0.15 pound Caramel 60 malt

*all grains should be milled (see note, page 17)

### 60-MINUTE BOIL

0.3 ounce Styrian Golding hops, divided into thirds

0.25 pound clear Belgian Candi Sugar (see note, page 22)

### FERMENT

½ packet Belgian ale yeast, such as Safale S-33 (see note, page 22)

3 tablespoons maple syrup, for bottling

**PREP:** The day before brewing, in a shallow tray, soak the oak chips in the bourbon at room temperature. Keep covered overnight.

**MASH:** In a medium stockpot, heat the 2¼ quarts water over high heat to 160°F. Add all the malts and stir gently. The temperature should reduce to 150°F within 1 minute. Turn off the heat. Steep the grains for 60 minutes between 144°F and 152°F. Every 10 minutes, stir and take the temperature. If the grains get too cold, turn on the heat to high while stirring until the temperature rises to that range, then turn off the heat. With 10 minutes left, in a second medium stockpot heat the 1 gallon water to 170°F. After the grains have steeped for 60 minutes, raise the heat of the grains-and-water mixture to high and stir until the temperature reaches 170°F. Turn off the heat.

**SPARGE:** Place a fine-mesh strainer over a pot, and pour the grains into the strainer, reserving the liquid. Pour the 1 gallon of 170°F water over the grains. Recirculate the collected liquid through the grains once.

**BOIL:** Return the pot with the liquid to the stove on high heat and bring to a boil. When it starts to foam, reduce the heat to a slow rolling boil. Add one third of the Styrian Golding hops after 30 minutes, 55 minutes, and 59 minutes. At the 60-minute mark, turn off the heat, add the oak chips, bourbon, and the Belgian Candi Sugar, and stir to dissolve the sugar. Prepare an ice bath by stopping the sink and filling it with 5 inches of water and ice. Place the pot in the ice bath in the sink and cool to 70°F, about 30 minutes.

**FERMENT:** Using a sanitized funnel and strainer, pour the liquid into a sanitized fermenter. Add any water needed to fill the jug to the 1-gallon mark. Add the yeast, sanitize your hands, cover the mouth of the jug with one hand, and shake to distribute evenly. Attach a sanitized stopper and tubing to the fermenter and insert the other end of the tubing into a small bowl of sanitizing solution. The solution will begin to bubble as the yeast activates, pushing gas through the tube. Wait 2 to 3 days until the bubbling has slowed, then replace the tubing system with an airlock (see page 28). Wait 11 more days, then bottle, using the maple syrup (see page 30 for bottling instructions).

## FOR 5 GALLONS

**Prep: 3.75 ounces oak chips; 1²/₃ cups bourbon**

**60-minute mash at 152°F: 3 gallons water, plus 5 gallons for sparging; 8.5 pounds Belgian Pilsner malt, 1.25 pounds Munich malt, 1 pound Special B malt, 0.75 pound Caramel 60 malt**

**60-minute boil: 1.5 ounce Styrian Golding hops, divided into thirds; 1.25 pounds clear Belgian Candi Sugar**

**Ferment: 1 packet Belgian ale yeast, such as Safale S-33; 1 cup maple syrup, for bottling**

## SUGGESTED FOOD PAIRINGS

- **Peking duck**
- **Yams**
- **Mashed potatoes**

# SUMMER WHEAT BEERS CAN HAVE A TART, CRISP FRESHNESS.

For a dark winter wheat, when you want a weightier mouth feel and substance, choosing the right style of yeast is very important. The one we use here helps bring out banana and bubble-gum aromas and heightens frothiness. The result is deep and rich, with a malty finish.

# WINTER WHEAT
## 5.5% ABV

### 60-MINUTE MASH AT 152°F

2 quarts water, plus 1 gallon for sparging

1.36 pounds Pale Wheat malt

0.5 pound Munich malt

0.2 pound Biscuit malt

0.1 pound Special B malt

*all grains should be milled (see note, page 17)

### 60-MINUTE BOIL

0.15 ounce Spaltz hops, divided into thirds

0.04 ounce Sorachi hops

### FERMENT

½ packet German wheat ale yeast, such as Wyeast Bavarian Wheat Blend (see note, page 22)

3 tablespoons honey, for bottling

**MASH:** In a medium stockpot, heat the 2 quarts water over high heat to 160°F. Add all the malts and stir gently. The temperature should reduce to 150°F within 1 minute. Turn off the heat and cover. Steep the grains for 60 minutes between 144°F and 152°F. Every 10 minutes, stir and take the temperature. If the grains get too cold, turn on the heat to high while stirring until the temperature rises to that range, then turn off the heat. With 10 minutes left, in a second medium stockpot heat the 1 gallon water to 170°F. After the grains have steeped for 60 minutes, raise the heat of the grains-and-water mixture to high and stir until the temperature reaches 170°F. Turn off the heat.

**SPARGE:** Place a fine-mesh strainer over a pot, and pour the grains into the strainer, reserving the liquid. Pour the 1 gallon of 170°F water over the grains. Recirculate the collected liquid through the grains once.

**BOIL:** Return the pot with the liquid to the stove on high heat and bring to a boil. When it starts to foam, reduce the heat to a slow rolling boil and add two thirds of the Spaltz hops. Add the remaining Spaltz hops after 30 minutes, and the Sorachi hops after 50 minutes. Prepare an ice bath by stopping the sink and filling it with 5 inches of water and ice. At the 60-minute mark, turn off the heat. Place the pot in the ice bath in the sink and cool to 70°F, about 30 minutes.

**FERMENT:** Using a sanitized funnel and strainer, pour the liquid into a sanitized fermenter. Add any water needed to fill the jug to the 1-gallon mark. Add the yeast, sanitize your hands, cover the mouth of the jug with one hand, and shake to distribute evenly. Attach a sanitized stopper and tubing to the fermenter and insert the other end of the tubing into a small bowl of sanitizing solution. The solution will begin to bubble as the yeast activates, pushing gas through the tube. Wait 2 to 3 days until the bubbling has slowed, then replace the tubing system with an airlock (see page 28). Wait 11 more days, then bottle, using the honey (see page 30 for bottling instructions).

## FOR 5 GALLONS

**60-minute mash at 152°F: 2½ gallons water, plus 5 gallons for sparging; 6.8 pounds Pale Wheat malt, 2.5 pounds Munich malt, 1 pound Biscuit malt, 0.5 pound Special B malt**

**60-minute boil: 0.75 ounce Spaltz hops, divided into thirds; 0.2 ounce Sorachi hops**

**Ferment: 1 packet German wheat ale yeast, such as Wyeast Bavarian Wheat Blend; 1 cup honey, for bottling**

- - - - - - - - - - - - - - -

## SUGGESTED FOOD PAIRINGS

- **Roasted root vegetables**
- **Roasted fish**
- **Bitter salads**

# IN THIS BREAKFAST STOUT,

the coffee flavor of roasted malt is amplified by the addition of real coffee beans, while coconut flakes, yeast, and grain form the components of a deconstructed donut. It's a great pour for brunch: The softness of the coconut tempers the sharpness of the bitter dark grains and coffee. We highly recommend this when it's snowing outside.

# COFFEE & DONUT STOUT 6.8% ABV

### 60-MINUTE MASH AT 152°F

2¼ quarts water, plus 1 gallon for sparging

1.5 pounds Pale Ale malt

0.3 pound Caramel 40 malt

0.2 pound Caramel 120 malt

0.1 pound Chocolate malt

0.1 pound roasted barley

0.1 pound flaked oats

*all grains should be milled (see note, page 17)

### 60-MINUTE BOIL

0.3 ounce Challenger hops, divided into sixths

½ cup flaked unsweetened coconut

¼ cup coffee beans, crushed

⅓ cup packed light brown sugar

### FERMENT

½ packet Belgian ale yeast, such as Safale S-33 (see note, page 22)

3 tablespoons maple syrup, for bottling

**MASH:** In a medium stockpot, heat 2¼ quarts water over high heat to 160°F. Add all the malts, barley, and oats and stir gently. The temperature should reduce to 150°F within 1 minute. Turn off the heat. Steep the grains for 60 minutes between 144°F and 152°F. Every 10 minutes, stir and take the temperature. If the grains get too cold, turn on the heat to high while stirring until the temperature rises to that range, then turn off the heat. With 10 minutes left, in a second medium stockpot heat the 1 gallon water to 170°F. After the grains have steeped for 60 minutes, raise the heat of the grains-and-water mixture to high and stir until the temperature reaches 170°F. Turn off the heat.

**SPARGE:** Place a fine-mesh strainer over a pot, and pour the grains into the strainer, reserving the liquid. Pour the 1 gallon of 170°F water over the grains. Recirculate the collected liquid through the grains once.

**BOIL:** Return the pot with the liquid to the stove on high heat and bring to a boil. When it starts to foam, reduce the heat to a slow rolling boil and add two sixths (one third) of the Challenger hops. Add one sixth of the Challenger hops after 15 minutes and 30 minutes, the flaked coconut after 40 minutes, another one sixth of the hops after 45 minutes, the coffee beans after 50 minutes, and the remaining hops after 55 minutes. Prepare an ice bath by stopping the sink and filling it with 5 inches of water and ice. At the 60-minute mark, turn off the heat, add the brown sugar, and stir to dissolve. Place the pot in the ice bath in the sink and cool to 70°F, about 30 minutes.

**FERMENT:** Using a sanitized funnel and strainer, pour the liquid into a sanitized fermenter. Add any water needed to fill the jug to the 1-gallon mark. Add the yeast, sanitize your hands, cover the mouth of the jug with one hand, and shake to distribute evenly. Attach a sanitized stopper and tubing to the fermenter and insert the other end of the tubing into a small bowl of sanitizing solution. The solution will begin to bubble as the yeast activates, pushing gas through the tube. Wait 2 to 3 days until the bubbling has slowed, then replace the tubing system with an airlock (see page 28). Wait 11 more days, then bottle, using the maple syrup (see page 30 for bottling instructions).

## FOR 5 GALLONS

**60-minute mash at 152°F: 3 gallons water, plus 5 gallons for sparging; 7.5 pounds Pale Ale malt, 1.5 pounds Caramel 40 malt, 1 pound Caramel 120 malt, 0.5 pound Chocolate malt, 0.5 pound roasted barley, 0.5 pound flaked oats**

**60-minute boil: 1.5 ounces Challenger hops, divided into sixths; 2½ cups flaked unsweetened coconut; 1¼ cups coffee beans, crushed; 1²/₃ cups packed light brown sugar**

**Ferment: 1 packet Belgian ale yeast, such as Safale S-33; 1 cup maple syrup, for bottling**

- - - - - - - - - - - - - - -

## SUGGESTED FOOD PAIRINGS

- **Donuts**
- **Coffee cakes**
- **Spice-rubbed roasts**

**FOR CHRISTMAS, WHEN ERICA WAS A KID,** her mom would make dates stuffed with buttercream frosting and rolled in sugar—the sweetest snack on earth. When we set out to make a light dessert beer, the idea of adding layers of natural sweeteners— dates and honey—just seemed right for the style and the season. Honey helps to build body, while dates have lots of sugar but also a distinct caramel-like flavor. Use the plump Medjool variety if you can find them, but varieties like Deglet Noor are great, too.

# DATES & HONEY ALE 4.7% ABV

### 60-MINUTE MASH AT 152°F

1¾ quarts water, plus 1 gallon for sparging

1.2 pounds Belgian Pilsner malt

0.2 pound Caramel 20 malt

0.2 pound Biscuit malt

*all grains should be milled (see note, page 17)

### 60-MINUTE BOIL

0.1 ounce Columbus hops

0.3 ounce Citra hops, divided into thirds

3 large dates, chopped

⅓ cup honey

### FERMENT

½ packet Belgian ale yeast, such Safale S-33 (see note, page 22)

3 tablespoons honey, for bottling

**MASH:** In a medium stockpot, heat the 1¾ quarts water over high heat to 160°F. Add all the malts and stir gently. The temperature should reduce to 150°F within 1 minute. Turn off the heat. Steep the grains for 60 minutes between 144°F and 152°F. Every 10 minutes, stir and take the temperature. If the grains get too cold, turn on the heat to high while stirring until the temperature rises to that range, then turn off the heat. With 10 minutes left, in a second medium stockpot heat the 1 gallon water to 170°F. After the grains have steeped for 60 minutes, raise the heat of the grains-and-water mixture to high and stir until the temperature reaches 170°F. Turn off the heat.

**SPARGE:** Place a fine-mesh strainer over a pot, and pour the grains into the strainer, reserving the liquid. Pour the 1 gallon of 170°F water over the grains. Recirculate the collected liquid through the grains once.

**BOIL:** Return the pot with the liquid to the stove on high heat and bring to a boil. When it starts to foam, reduce the heat to a slow rolling boil and add the Columbus hops. Add one third of the Citra hops after 30 minutes, and another third of the Citra hops and all of the dates after 45 minutes. At the 60-minute mark, turn off the heat, add the remaining Citra hops and the ⅓ cup honey, and stir to combine. Prepare an ice bath by stopping the sink and filling it with 5 inches of water and ice. Place the pot in the ice bath in the sink and cool to 70°F, about 30 minutes.

**FERMENT:** Using a sanitized funnel and strainer, pour the liquid into a sanitized fermenter. Add any water needed to fill the jug to the 1-gallon mark. Add the yeast, sanitize your hands, cover the mouth of the jug with one hand, and shake to distribute evenly. Attach a sanitized stopper and tubing to the fermenter and insert the other end of the tubing into a small bowl of sanitizing solution. The solution will begin to bubble as the yeast activates, pushing gas through the tube. Wait 2 to 3 days until the bubbling has slowed, then replace the tubing system with an airlock (see page 28). Wait 11 more days, then bottle, using the 3 tablespoons honey (see page 30 for bottling instructions).

## FOR 5 GALLONS

**60-minute mash at 152°F: 2¼ gallons water, plus 5 gallons for sparging; 6 pounds Belgian Pilsner malt, 1 pound Caramel 20 malt, 1 pound Biscuit malt**

**60-minute boil: 0.5 ounce Columbus hops; 1.5 ounces Cltra hops, divided into thirds; 15 large dates, chopped; 1⅔ cups honey**

**Ferment: 1 packet Belgian ale yeast, such as Safale S-33; 1 cup honey, for bottling**

## SUGGESTED FOOD PAIRINGS

- **Honey-based desserts**
- **Ice cream**
- **Sheep's-milk cheese or aged goat cheese**

# TRADITIONAL BELGIAN ALES ARE OFTEN BREWED WITH ORANGE PEEL AND CORIANDER,

and they remain perennial favorites among beer lovers; they never go out of style. In the winter, however, when tiny clementines arrive in markets by the crate, we like to swap them in for regular oranges—they're sweeter and more aromatic. It's also a nice thematic twist for a New Year's celebration: a nod to the traditions of the past, but also a toast to the future. This light-bodied but high-alcohol ale works equally well for clinking glasses when the ball drops at midnight and for brunching the next day.

# NEW YEAR BEER 8.0% ABV

## PREP

2 clementines

## 60-MINUTE MASH AT 152°F

2¾ quarts water, plus 1 gallon for sparging

1.6 pounds Belgian Pilsner malt

0.6 pound Pale Wheat malt

0.3 pound Caramel 10 malt

0.2 pound Munich malt

*all grains should be milled (see note, page 17)

## 60-MINUTE BOIL

0.07 ounce Centennial hops

0.12 ounce Tettnanger hops

1 teaspoon coriander seeds

0.2 ounce Amarillo hops, divided into halves

0.3 pound clear Belgian Candi Sugar (see note, page 22)

## FERMENT

½ packet Belgian ale yeast, such as Wyeast Belgian Strong (see note, page 22)

3 tablespoons honey, for bottling

**PREP:** Peel the clementines, reserving the peels to dry out.

**MASH:** In a medium stockpot, heat the 2¾ quarts water over high heat to 160°F. Add all the malts and stir gently. The temperature should reduce to 150°F within 1 minute. Turn off the heat. Steep the grains for 60 minutes between 144°F and 152°F. Every 10 minutes, stir and take the temperature. If the grains get too cold, turn on the heat to high while stirring until the temperature rises to that range, then turn off the heat. With 10 minutes left, in a second medium stockpot heat the 1 gallon water to 170°F. After the grains have steeped for 60 minutes, raise the heat of the grains-and-water mixture to high and stir until the temperature reaches 170°F. Turn off the heat.

**SPARGE:** Place a fine-mesh strainer over a pot, and pour the grains into the strainer, reserving the liquid. Pour the 1 gallon of 170°F water over the grains. Recirculate the collected liquid through the grains once.

**BOIL:** Return the pot with the liquid to the stove on high heat and bring to a boil. When it starts to foam, reduce the heat to a slow rolling boil and add the Centennial hops. Add the Tettnanger hops after 30 minutes, the coriander after 50 minutes, and half of the Amarillo hops along with the clementine peels after 55 minutes. Prepare an ice bath by stopping the sink and filling it with 5 inches of water and ice. At the 60-minute mark, turn off the heat, add the remaining Amarillo hops and the Belgian Candi Sugar, and stir to dissolve the sugar. Place the pot in the ice bath in the sink and cool to 70°F, about 30 minutes.

**FERMENT:** Using a sanitized funnel and strainer, pour the liquid into a sanitized fermenter. Add any water needed to fill the jug to the 1-gallon mark. Add the yeast, sanitize your hands, cover the mouth of the jug with one hand, and shake to distribute evenly. Attach a sanitized stopper and tubing to the fermenter and insert the other end of the tubing into a small bowl of sanitizing solution. The solution will begin to bubble as the yeast activates, pushing gas through the tube. Wait 2 to 3 days until the bubbling has slowed, then replace the tubing system with an airlock (see page 28). Wait 11 more days, then bottle, using the honey (see page 30 for bottling instructions).

## FOR 5 GALLONS

**Prep: 10 clementines**

**60-minute mash at 152°F:** 3½ gallons water, plus 5 gallons for sparging; 8 pounds Belgian Pilsner malt, 3 pounds Pale Wheat malt, 1.5 pounds Caramel 10 malt, 1 pound Munich malt

**60-minute boil:** 0.35 ounce Centennial hops; 0.5 ounce Tettnanger hops; 2 tablespoons coriander seeds; 1 ounce Amarillo hops, divided into halves; 1.5 pounds clear Belgian Candi Sugar

**Ferment:** 1 packet Belgian ale yeast, such as Wyeast Belgian Strong; 1 cup honey, for bottling

- - - - - - - - - - - - - -

## SUGGESTED FOOD PAIRINGS

- **Macaroons**
- **Moule frites**
- **Soft mild cheeses**

# EGGNOG DRAWS A STRONG REACTION FROM PEOPLE: EITHER THEY LOVE IT OR THEY HATE IT.

For some, it's a once-a-year indulgence that conjures images of frothy punch bowls and snifters by the fireplace. For others, it's that weird cardboard carton that shows up in the milk aisle in December. Erica is in the first camp: She loves it. Her parents used to throw huge parties around the holidays and they would make giant batches of the *Joy of Cooking* eggnog recipe and put cauldrons of it out in the snow to chill.

When we were playing with the idea of making a dark rich milk stout for the holidays, an eggnog version was a natural leap. There isn't actual milk in the beer, but the addition of lactose sugar makes it taste creamy and full-bodied. Since the sugar doesn't convert to alcohol, the residual sweetness tempers the bitterness common in stouts while enhancing the roasted barley flavor. Here, a vanilla bean and some freshly grated nutmeg bring out all the right eggnoggy aromas, and a creamy head from a Belgian strain of yeast completes the picture.

# EGGNOG MILK STOUT 5.8% ABV

## 60-MINUTE MASH AT 152°F

2 quarts water, plus 1 gallon for sparging

1.4 pounds English Pale malt

0.2 pound Caramel 60 malt

0.1 pound Chocolate malt

0.2 pound roasted barley

*all grains should be milled (see note, page 17)

## 60-MINUTE BOIL

0.2 ounce Northern Brewer hops, divided into halves

½ whole nutmeg, grated

0.1 ounce Fuggle hops

0.2 pound lactose sugar

## FERMENT

½ packet Belgian ale yeast, such as Safale S-33 (see note, page 22)

½ vanilla bean

3 tablespoons maple syrup, for bottling

**MASH:** In a medium stockpot, heat the 2 quarts water over high heat to 160°F. Add all the malts and barley and stir gently. The temperature should reduce to 150°F within 1 minute. Turn off the heat. Steep the grains for 60 minutes between 144°F and 152°F. Every 10 minutes, stir and take the temperature. If the grains get too cold, turn on the heat to high while stirring until the temperature rises to that range, then turn off the heat. With 10 minutes left, in a second medium stockpot heat the 1 gallon water to 170°F. After the grains have steeped for 60 minutes, raise the heat of the grains-and-water mixture to high and stir until the temperature reaches 170°F. Turn off the heat.

**SPARGE:** Place a fine-mesh strainer over a pot, and pour the grains into the strainer, reserving the liquid. Pour the 1 gallon of 170°F water over the grains. Recirculate the collected liquid through the grains once.

**BOIL:** Return the pot with the liquid to the stove on high heat and bring to a boil. When it starts to foam, reduce the heat to a slow rolling boil and add half of the Northern Brewer hops. Add the remaining Northern Brewer hops and grated nutmeg after 30 minutes, and the Fuggle hops after 59 minutes. Prepare an ice bath by stopping the sink and filling it with 5 inches of water and ice. At the 60-minute mark, turn off the heat, add the lactose sugar, and stir to dissolve. Place the pot in the ice bath in the sink and cool to 70°F, about 30 minutes.

**RECIPE CONTINUES**

**FERMENT:** Using a sanitized funnel and strainer, pour the liquid into a sanitized fermenter. Add any water needed to fill the jug to the 1-gallon mark. Add the yeast, sanitize your hands, cover the mouth of the jug with one hand, and shake to distribute evenly. Attach a sanitized stopper and tubing to the fermenter and insert the other end of the tubing into a small bowl of sanitizing solution. The solution will begin to bubble as the yeast activates, pushing gas through the tube. Wait 2 to 3 days until the bubbling has slowed, then soak the ½ vanilla bean in ¼ cup boiling water for 90 seconds and add it to the fermenter. Replace the tubing system with an airlock (see page 28). Wait 11 more days, then bottle, using the maple syrup (see page 30 for bottling instructions).

**Note:** Stephen uses breakfast cereal as an excuse for drinking excessive quantities of milk, whereas Erica is lactose intolerant. It's her kryptonite. So be aware that if you're lactose intolerant, you should steer clear of this beer or make it without the lactose, and you'll have a rich stout with a hint of vanilla and nutmeg spice.

## FOR 5 GALLONS

**60-minute mash at 152°F:** 2½ gallons water, plus 5 gallons for sparging; 7 pounds English Pale malt, 1 pound Caramel 60 malt, 0.5 pound Chocolate malt, 1 pound roasted barley

**60-minute boil:** 1 ounce Northern Brewer hops, divided into halves; 2½ whole nutmegs, grated; 0.5 ounce Fuggle hops; 1 pound lactose sugar

**Ferment:** 1 packet Belgian ale yeast, such as Safale S-33; 3 vanilla beans; 1 cup maple syrup, for bottling

- - - - - - - - - - - - - - -

## SUGGESTED FOOD PAIRINGS

· **Cream desserts**
· **Sugar cookies**
· **Roasted meats**

# OUR GINGERBREAD ALE WAS AN IDEAL CANDIDATE TO BE RETOOLED AS GLUTEN-FREE.

Loads of warming baking spices and sweet candied ginger boost the flavor profile, and the addition of molasses, an ingredient found in American colonial beers when traditional grains were scarce, fits in perfectly with the concept.

# GLUTEN-FREE GINGER-BREAD ALE

3.5% ABV

**RECIPE CONTINUES**

## PREP

1½ pounds whole buckwheat (see note, page 93)

## 70-MINUTE MASH

1½ quarts water plus 1½ quarts, plus 1 gallon for sparging

0.2 pound rice hulls (see note, page 61)

0.5 pound red quinoa

## 60-MINUTE BOIL

0.2 ounce Centennial hops

3 whole cloves

1 cinnamon stick

1 teaspoon candied ginger

½ whole nutmeg, grated

0.1 ounce Hallertau hops

1 cup molasses

1 cup packed light brown sugar

## FERMENT

½ packet gluten-free yeast, such as Nottingham (see note, page 22)

3 tablespoons maple syrup, for bottling

**PREP:** Rinse the buckwheat, then cover in water and soak for 30 hours, changing the water and rinsing the grains every 8 hours. Strain, rinse once more, then leave the grains in a colander in the dark for 1 day, or until you see the grains begin to sprout. Let the grains sit until the sprouts have doubled in size, about 2 days. Preheat the oven to its lowest setting, or 200°F. Spread the grains over an unoiled rimmed baking sheet and bake for 60 minutes, or until the grains become dry. Rub the dried grains between your hands until the sprouted material falls away. Place the grains in a resealable plastic bag and crush with a rolling pin to "mill."

**MASH:** In a medium stockpot, heat the 1½ quarts water over high heat to 110°F. Add the buckwheat and stir gently. The temperature should drop to 95°F. Turn off the heat. Steep the grains for 15 minutes at 95°F, then turn the heat on high while stirring to raise the temperature to 113°F. Turn off the heat. Steep the grains for 15 minutes at 113°F, then add the rice hulls, an additional 1½ quarts water, and the quinoa and turn the heat on high while stirring to raise the temperature to 149°F. Steep the grains for 40 minutes at 149°F. Every 10 minutes, stir and take the temperature. If the grains get too cold, turn on the heat to high while stirring until the temperature rises to 149°F, then turn off the heat. With 10 minutes left, in a second medium stockpot heat the 1 gallon of water to 150°F.

**SPARGE:** Place a fine-mesh strainer over a pot, and pour the grains into the strainer, reserving the liquid. Pour the 1 gallon of 150°F water over the grains. Recirculate the collected liquid through the grains once.

**BOIL:** Return the pot with the liquid to the stove on high heat and bring to a boil. When it starts to foam, reduce the heat to a slow rolling boil and add the Centennial hops, whole cloves, and cinnamon stick. Add the candied ginger and nutmeg after 30 minutes and the Hallertau hops after 55 minutes. Prepare an ice bath by stopping the sink and filling it with 5 inches of water and ice. At the 60-minute mark, turn off the heat, add the molasses and sugar, and stir to dissolve. Place the pot in the ice bath in the sink and cool to 70°F, about 30 minutes.

**FERMENT:** Using a sanitized funnel and strainer, pour the liquid into a sanitized fermenter. Add any water needed to fill the jug to the 1-gallon mark. Add the gluten-free yeast, sanitize your hands, cover the mouth of the jug with one hand, and shake to distribute evenly. Attach a sanitized stopper and tubing to the fermenter and insert the other end of the tubing into a small bowl of sanitizing solution. The solution will begin to bubble as the yeast activates, pushing gas through the tube. Wait 2 to 3 days until the bubbling has slowed, then replace the tubing system with an airlock (see page 28). Wait 11 more days, then bottle, using the maple syrup (see page 30 for bottling instructions).

## FOR 5 GALLONS

**Prep: 7.5 pounds buckwheat**

**70-minute mash: 4 gallons water, plus 5 gallons for sparging; 0.5 pound rice hulls; 2.5 pounds red quinoa**

**60-minute boil: 1 ounce Centennial hops; 15 whole cloves; 3 cinnamon sticks; 2 tablespoons candied ginger; 2 whole nutmegs, grated; 0.5 ounce Hallertau hops; 5 cups molasses; 5 cups light brown sugar**

**Ferment: 1 packet gluten-free yeast, such as Nottingham; 1 cup maple syrup, for bottling**

- - - - - - - - - - - - - -

## SUGGESTED FOOD PAIRINGS

- **Vanilla ice cream**
- **Crème brûlée**
- **Banana splits**

# BEER & CARAMEL
# POPCORN

This gussied-up version of something you'd find at a ballpark is a great snack to have on hand for a holiday party, or wrap it up and give it as a gift. Most of the ingredients are things you might already have in your cupboards. We discovered how handy that was when we were prepping for a holiday party we didn't have time to plan. After our kits were featured on a segment of *Live with Regis and Kelly* in the morning, our website received so much traffic it crashed three times, leading us to spend the day taking orders by phone with no time to cook for our party. So we ended up only having a cheese platter and this popcorn. Nobody minded.

**SERVES 6 to 8**

1½ cups raw peanuts

1 cup beer, such as Gingerbread Ale (page 142), Eggnog Milk Stout (page 160), or Peanut Butter Porter (page 110)

1 cup sugar

¼ cup agave syrup

6 tablespoons (¾ stick) unsalted butter, cut into tablespoons

¾ teaspoon baking soda

8 cups popped popcorn (made from ⅓ cup kernels)

Vegetable oil

- - - - - - - - - - - - - - - - - - - - - - - - - - - - - - - - - - - - - - - - -

In a medium skillet, cook the peanuts over medium-high heat until toasted, about 3 minutes. Set aside. In a medium heavy-bottomed saucepan, heat the beer over medium-high heat until it boils. Cook until it reduces to ¼ cup, about 10 minutes. Add the sugar and agave syrup and continue to cook until the mixture reaches 300°F, or until it is thick and bubbly. Add the butter, 1 tablespoon at a time, stirring constantly. Add the baking soda and stir to dissolve. The mixture will foam.

Place the popcorn in a large, well-oiled bowl, pour the caramel evenly over the top, then sprinkle on the peanuts. Toss together with tongs or a wooden spoon until evenly coated. Spread on a well-oiled rimmed baking sheet and cool until the caramel has hardened, about 60 minutes.

# BEER & SAGE FONDUE

**NOTE:** FOR BEST RESULTS, YOU'LL NEED A FONDUE POT OR A DOUBLE BOILER.

This is a perfect warming party dish for a winter get-together. Stephen bought an antique copper fondue pot from 1896 for Erica's birthday in the days before the Brooklyn Brew Shop and it still makes an appearance several times each winter. Serve this with toasted bread on skewers and a nice Belgian ale, such as our Honey Sage Seasonal.

**SERVES 8 as a light main course**

1 garlic clove, peeled and smashed

1½ cups plus 2 tablespoons beer, such as Honey Sage Seasonal (see page 144)

2 cups grated Gruyère cheese

2 cups grated Emmentaler cheese

1 tablespoon all-purpose flour

1 teaspoon finely chopped fresh sage

Freshly ground black pepper

---

Rub the garlic clove around the inside of a fondue pot or top half of a double boiler. Add 1½ cups of the beer and heat over medium-high heat until boiling. Add the Gruyère and Emmentaler cheeses ¼ cup at a time, alternating between the two and stirring to melt.

Whisk the flour and the remaining beer into the fondue, reduce the heat to low, and let the simmering mixture thicken, about 5 minutes. Stir in the sage and season with pepper to taste. Serve hot.

# BEER ICE CREAM FLOAT

Winter beers make delicious, rich ice cream floats. Serve them for dessert after dinner or as a late-night cocktail. Here are some of our favorite combinations:

- CHOCOLATE MAPLE PORTER (page 138) and CHOCOLATE ICE CREAM
- BOURBON DUBBEL (page 150) and CARAMEL SWIRL ICE CREAM
- EGGNOG MILK STOUT (page 160) and FRENCH VANILLA ICE CREAM
- COFFEE & DONUT STOUT (page 154) and ROCKY ROAD ICE CREAM

**SERVES 1**

1 scoop of ice cream
1 bottle of beer

- - - - - - - - - - - - - - - - - - - - - - - - - - - - - - - - - - - - - - - - - -

Drop the scoop of ice cream into a tall glass. Slowly pour the beer over the ice cream, being careful not to let the beer foam over. Serve with a long spoon.

**Variation:** Instead of ice cream try filling half a glass with Gingerbread Ale (page 142) and topping with eggnog and freshly grated nutmeg for a super-rich holiday treat.

# SPENT-GRAIN DOG BISCUITS

Once you've made your beer, the question remains: What should you do with the spent grain? Many breweries donate theirs to farms for animal feed. We use ours to make biscuits for all the cute dogs who come to the Brooklyn Flea Market on weekends. You can get creative with the shapes. We like to make ours in the shape of mini dog bones.

**MAKES 12 biscuits**

2 cups spent grain

1 cup all-purpose flour

1 cup creamy natural peanut butter

½ cup pumpkin puree (from a can or from roasted fresh pumpkin)

1 egg

---

Preheat the oven to 375°F. In a large bowl, combine the spent grain, flour, peanut butter, pumpkin puree, and egg. Roll the mixture into twelve 2-inch balls. Grease a baking sheet with cooking spray and place the balls on the sheet, about 2 inches apart.

Flatten the balls to ¾-inch height and bake them for 30 minutes. Lower the heat to 225°F and cook until they are dry, about 8 hours.

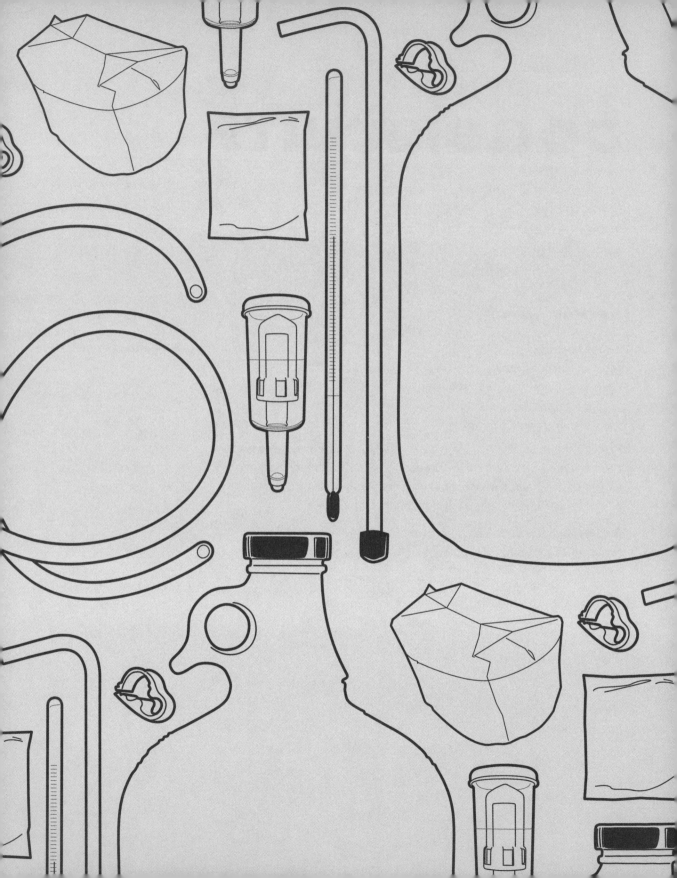

# ACKNOWLEDGMENTS

To our customers who saw a bag of grain and a jug and knew they had to make some beer. A love for taking on new projects is what got us into brewing and then into starting a company. We call the beers in this book ours, but really they are yours.

To Eric Demby and the Brooklyn Flea—the market that launched our business and the artisan food vendors who still inspire us, feed us, and remind us we're not crazy for quitting our jobs and starting a company.

To Tim Evans, whose dedication, talent, and adaptability make everything work and because a third person in the room makes it a real business.

To Deryck Vonn Lee—an absolutely brilliant designer, illustrator, and friend.

To our agent, Bob Mecoy, and co-writer, Jennifer Fiedler, who helped turn our beers into a book. And to Gabe Soria for making all the right introductions.

To Emily Takoudes, Peggy Paul, and everyone at Clarkson Potter for making this whole process the least stressful part of running a hectic company.

To Jeff Wallace for making our first retail customer a Whole Foods in New York City and to all the wonderful stores that have since welcomed our kit to their shelves and helped shoppers around the country become brewers.

To our friends, volunteers, and total strangers who helped us get through our first two holiday seasons. We owe you all a lot of beer.

To Erica's parents, who drink, and to Stephen's, who do not. And to our brothers and sisters. Thank you for your continuous love and support.

To Stephen. Without you, I'd be an astronaut.

To Erica. Without you, I'd eat at a lot fewer restaurants.

# SOURCES

## BREWING SUPPLY STORES

### BROOKLYN BREW SHOP

brooklynbrewshop.com
info@brooklynbrewshop.com
One-gallon kits, equipment, ingredient mixes

Brooklyn Brew Shop ingredient mixes and kits are also available at Whole Foods Markets, Williams-Sonoma, West Elm, and specialty stores nationwide. For a full list of retailers, see brooklynbrewshop.com/locator.

### HOME BREWERS ASSOCIATION

homebrewersassociation.org
Listings of local brewing supply shops, competitions, classes, and meet-ups

### MIDWEST SUPPLIES

midwestsupplies.com
General brewing equipment, brewing ingredients

### NORTHERN BREWER

northernbrewer.com
General brewing equipment, brewing ingredients

## SPECIALTY INGREDIENT STORES

### HARNEY & SONS

harney.com
Tea

### KALUSTYAN'S

kalustyans.com
Spices, teas, and specialty foods

### NUTS ONLINE

nutsonline.com
Nuts, nut butters, whole buckwheat

### SPICE STATION

spicestationsilverlake.com
Spices

### STUMPTOWN COFFEE

stumptowncoffee.com
Coffee

### TAZA CHOCOLATE

tazachocolate.com
Chocolate fines

### WHOLE FOODS MARKETS (multiple locations nationwide)

wholefoodsmarket.com
Spices, gluten-free grains, specialty foods

## SEASONAL PRODUCE

### GROW NYC

grownyc.org
New York City farmer's markets

### FRESHOPS

freshhops.com
Purveyors of fine hops

### JUST FOOD

justfood.org
Local New York City produce

### LOCAL HARVEST

localharvest.org
Listings of local farmer's markets across the United States

# GLOSSARY

**ABV (ALCOHOL BY VOLUME):** measurement of how much alcohol is in a liquid, expressed as a percentage

**ALPHA ACID:** compound found in hops that adds bitterness to beer

**ATTENUATION:** amount of sugars that yeast consume during fermentation, expressed as a percentage

**CARBOY:** glass fermenter used in brewing

**CARBOY BUNG:** rubber stopper used to seal a carboy

**DUBBEL:** strong, malty Belgian ale

**DUNKEL:** dark German lager

**DUNKELWEISEN:** dark German wheat beer

**ESTER:** compound responsible for fruity aromas in beer

**FLOCCULATION:** process during fermentation in which yeast particles clump together and fall to the bottom of the fermenter to form the trub

**GOSE:** sour-wheat-beer style that originated in the town of Goslar, Germany

**GROWLERS:** small refillable jugs used to transport beer from a tap

**HEFEWEIZEN:** unfiltered German wheat beer that is typically slightly cloudy

**PHYNOL:** compound created by some yeast strains or by using highly chlorinated water that produces spicy or rubber aromas in beer

**RAUCHBIER:** smoked German beer that gets its character from malted barley that has been smoked

**REINHEITSGEBOT:** German Beer Purity law passed in 1516 that limited the ingredients used in the production of beer to barley, hops, and water

**SAISON(S):** fruity Belgian style of ale traditionally brewed at warmer temperatures of up to 95°F

**SPARGE:** meaning "to sprinkle" in brewing, refers to the process of pouring hot water over strained grains to extract the maximum amount of sugars from the grains

**SPARGING BAG:** nylon mesh bag used to strain grains in the sparge step

**TORRIFIED WHEAT:** kernels of wheat that have been heated until they puff up and are used when brewing in small amounts to add body to the beer and achieve better head retention

**TRUB:** layer of sediment that gathers at the bottom of the fermenter during fermentation

**WEISSE BEER:** a German wheat beer

**WORT:** sugary liquid collected from straining the grains out of the mash

# INDEX